HAMPSHIRE
and **D-DAY**

HAMPSHIRE and **D-DAY**

Editor
Martin Doughty
Contributors
Ken Ford
Martin Polley
Alastair Wilson
Lesley Burton
Ann Bailey
Michael Hughes
Stephen Brooks

HAMPSHIRE BOOKS

First published in 1994 by Hampshire Books
Copyright © 1994 Hampshire County Council

HAMPSHIRE BOOKS
Official Publisher to

 Hampshire
COUNTY COUNCIL

in association with Southgate Publishers Ltd

Southgate Publishers Ltd
Glebe House, Church Street, Crediton, Devon EX17 2AF
Tel: 0363 777575 Fax: 0363 776007

SALES
Direct sales enquiries to Hampshire Books at the address above.

ISBN 1–85741–047–5

British Library Cataloguing-in-publication Data
CIP Catalogue Record for this book is available from the British Library

Printed and bound in Great Britain by Short Run Press Ltd,
Exeter, Devon.

Front cover: Portsmouth – prelude to D-Day. Artist: Bill Bishop (Courtesy
of the Trustees of the Royal Naval Museum, Portsmouth.)

CONTENTS

ACKNOWLEDGEMENTS

This project owes its inception to the vision and foresight of General Sir Hugh Beach, Maldwin Drummond of Cadland and, above all, Councillor F.A.J. Emery-Wallis, former Leader of Hampshire County Council and tireless champion of local history in the county and elsewhere. Lord Montagu of Beaulieu also provided support.

The book would not have been written without the commitment and enthusiasm of Ann Bailey, who worked as Research Assistant and contributed to it. The Editor would like to thank the contributors and owes a special debt of gratitude to Sarah Lewin and Rosemary Dunhill of Hampshire Record Office and to Simon Goodenough and the staff of Southgate Publishers. Thanks are also due to Jill Gill of the Beaulieu Archive for making Mrs Borthwick's reminiscences available to us and to Bill Johnson of the University of Portsmouth Geography Department for drawing the maps.

The staff of the following institutions provided invaluable assistance with research and photographic materials: Hampshire County Library Service; Hampshire Record Office, Winchester; Imperial War Museum, London; Martial Rose Library, King Alfred's College, Winchester; The Public Record Office, Kew; Southampton City Record Office; Southern Tourist Board, Eastleigh; Wessex Film and Sound Archive, Winchester; the *Naval Review*.

Finally, we would all like to thank the people of Hampshire whose reminiscences form so large a part of the book. In particular: Mrs D. Allen, Mr S. Ashley, Mr P. Barfield, Mr G. Bartlett, Mrs P. Borthwick, Mrs C. Bradley, Miss S. Brewster, Mr J. Byrne, Mrs S. Clarke, Mrs I. Clements, Mrs N.A. Cox, Mr W. Earley, Mrs D. Elliott, Mr S. Gamble, Mrs M.L. Giles, Cmdr J. Goulding R.N., Mr A.G. Greer, Mr & Mrs B. Grey, Squadron Ldr Frank Hayward, Mr T.R. Hiett, Mrs P. Hodges, Mr P. Jeffries, Mr & Mrs R.R. Lee, Mr I. Marshall, Mr R.A. Marshall, Mr M.J. Masson, Mrs V. Maunder, Mr D. Mortimore, Mr A. Page, Mr R. Pavey, Mr A.J.C. Reger, Mr E.G. Richards, Mr P. Vince, Mrs A. Wilkinson, Mrs E.W. Wright.

Councillor Mike Hancock CBE, Leader
of Hampshire County Council

The invasion of Europe which began on 6th June 1944 involved one of the largest concentrations of military, naval and air power the world has ever seen. Behind every Allied soldier who set foot in Normandy and the naval and air forces which supported and supplied him was a vast logistical effort which involved many nations and spanned continents. Yet, in the end, this immense force was projected to the far shore through the relatively small area of southern England and, in particular, Hampshire.

Hampshire, both because of its geography – its position directly opposite the beaches of Normandy – and its historical importance for Britain's naval and military power, became central to the success of the entire operation. Its ports and naval bases supplied the ships and the places from which to launch them and its roads and railways transported the troops, their vehicles and supplies. In addition, its ordinary people supported Operation OVERLORD in countless ways in their normal working lives, providing vital services and communications and helping to create essential equipment such as the famous MULBERRY floating harbours.

Using historical sources from Hampshire and London and the words and photographs of Hampshire people, this book tells the story of the D-Day operations. It describes the role of Hampshire as the command post for OVERLORD, the county's industrial, military and naval contributions and the effect these had on the lives of its ordinary citizens.

It is for the reasons above that Hampshire County Council is proud to be associated with this publication. We hope that this book offers a lasting tribute to those men and women who gave so much in that endless summer of 1944; that those of us having the opportunity of reading this book now and in the years to come have the chance to remember their commitment, dedication and sacrifice.

HAMPSHIRE'S UNIQUE CONTRIBUTION

Martin Doughty

Of all the events of the Second World War, the landing of Allied forces in Normandy on D-Day, 6th June 1944, has attracted special attention. Partly this reflects the size and complexity of the operation, codenamed OVERLORD, which involved amphibious, naval and air operations on an unprecedented scale. Partly, also, it reflects the very special significance for Allied morale of the opening of the 'second front' and the clarity with which, even at the time, D-Day was seen as marking the beginning of the end of a conflict which had already lasted nearly five years.

This book does not attempt to be a conventional account of the military history of D-Day. Instead, its focus is on a single county, Hampshire. Hampshire has been described as the 'springboard' for OVERLORD: the majority of the troops who took part in the operation left from Hampshire camps and Hampshire ports and were escorted by ships and aircraft based in the county. This is not to denigrate the contributions of other counties but merely to assert the fact that geography, and Hampshire's traditional connections with the fighting services, gave it a unique significance in the mounting of the operation.

In exploring that significance, we have concentrated on Hampshire and its people, rather than recounted the well-known facts of the military operations. We have focused on the ways in which Hampshire played a critical role in the economic and industrial preparations and through this have examined the experience of D-Day from the point of view of ordinary men and women. The book investigates the vital contribution of the county's industries, especially its communications systems and ports, and shows the impact on the ordinary civilian life of the county of the massive build-up of military power necessary to ensure that OVERLORD would be a success.

We have given especial attention to recounting the story in the words of those who experienced it at the time, whether as Hampshire residents confronted with tanks and armoured vehicles at the roadside, or as part of the massive civilian labour force devoted to OVERLORD: building the MULBERRY harbours, working in the ammunition factories, the hospitals or loading or unloading the ships. We have also included a chapter devoted to reminiscences of servicemen and women who were stationed in Hampshire in the build-up to D-Day and whose insights into the people they met and their reactions to the transformation of their county into the world's largest military camp are unique and fascinating. Finally, there are chapters on what can still be seen in Hampshire today of the installations created to prepare for OVERLORD.

In this way, we tell the story of a people at war, focused on their participation in one of the most audacious military operations of this century, and we draw attention to the importance of the contribution of the men and women of Hampshire in ensuring the success of Operation OVERLORD: the enormous undertaking which marked the beginning of the liberation of Europe.

CHAPTER ONE

THE GRAND STRATEGY FOR D-DAY

Ken Ford

In June 1940, the last remnants of the ill-fated British Expeditionary Force were extricated from the French port of Dunkirk just hours before the enveloping German panzer troops reached the Channel. This defeated army was brought home to join the few reserve divisions that made up the defence of the nation against the inevitable Nazi invasion.

The scale of the disaster and the rapidity with which Allied forces had been overcome led military opinion to believe that there could be no return to the Continent until Hitler's war machine had been severely curtailed by air bombardment, economic blockade and mass insurrection in the occupied territories. Whilst planners concentrated on the defence of the United Kingdom, the defeat of Germany could only be realistically contemplated through these means. Nonetheless, the Prime Minister, Winston Churchill, insisted on seizing the initiative by raising a combined operations division with the sole intention of harassing the enemy at every opportunity.

These cross-Channel raids were good for morale but were by no means rehearsals for an invasion. At that time amphibious warfare was very much in its infancy. There were neither any developed tactical philosophy nor any specialised equipment available to support an assault from the sea. Up until 1940 there had been no need for it. Apart from the Gallipoli landings in the First World War, men and *matériel* associated with a seaborne invasion had been landed through undefended ports. In the past, the British Navy had been able to put men ashore faster than an enemy had been able to concentrate against them. The tragic lessons of Gallipoli had turned the military decidedly against landing troops over open beaches.

A full-scale seaborne invasion against a defended coastline was a new facet of war and one on which little serious discussion had taken place. In the 1920s, some consideration had been given to the possibilities of combined attack by naval, air and land forces and some specialised landing craft had been designed as a consequence but development and production was subsequently hampered by government financial restrictions.

In the 1930s, Japan's operations in China had seen the use of specially constructed assault ships and landing craft. Understandably, both British and American military observers were interested in these moves. In response, the British set up an 'Inter-Service Training and Development Centre' at the Royal Marines' barracks at Eastney in Hampshire to evaluate them, whilst the USA, with its majority opinion holding an isolationist attitude to foreign military ventures, put little effort into the development of amphibious equipment.

In the period after Dunkirk, Britain was without any serious capability for launching a seaborne invasion against German held territory. However, the same was also true for Germany. When Hitler came to evolve his plans to land on the English coast, he found that his invasion force would have to land from merchant ships and barges.

Once ashore, he knew that the British Army was unlikely to be a match for his German panzer divisions. At sea, the picture was quite different. The Royal Navy was more than capable of defeating any seaborne armada, providing it had suitable air cover to protect its ships. This was the crux of the Battle of Britain: if the German Air Force could annihilate the Royal Air Force, then, unmolested, it could turn its attention to harassing the Royal Navy and allow the invasion fleet to land its troops.

The German Luftwaffe did not win the Battle of Britain and there was no invasion. Instead, Hitler turned his attention to the east and invaded Russia in June 1941. This respite from a threatened enemy landing enabled serious attention to be given to the possibility of a cross-Channel attack by Britain. Indeed, as German troops pushed deeper and deeper into Russia and Stalin's empire seemed close to collapse, the Russian leader felt that such a move would relieve some of the pressure felt by the communists.

Calls for this 'second front' continued to intensify as public sympathy for Russia's plight grew. Unfortunately, Britain was just as ill-prepared to launch a second front in 1941 as she was in 1940. There were just 37 equipped divisions in the UK in July 1941 compared to Germany's 250 mobilised divisions,

only 150 of which were involved in the attack on Russia. Worse still, enough landing craft had been built to transport only one brigade in a cross-Channel invasion. It was clear that a new 'second front' in Europe could not possibly take place until both sufficient troops and equipment were available to launch it and German forces had been considerably weakened by blockade, bombing and subversion. Churchill and his generals were convinced that peripheral operations against the fringes of the German territories, in such places as the Mediterranean and North Africa, was a more effective strategy with which to tie down German divisions.

Things changed somewhat in December 1941 when the USA was drawn into the war by the Japanese attack on Pearl Harbor in the Pacific. The Americans declared war on all Axis forces and agreed with Churchill that the European theatre of war would take priority over matters in the Far East. This 'Germany first' strategy would allow British, Russian and American forces to concentrate the bulk of their combat troops simultaneously against Hitler. President Roosevelt and his advisers joined with the Russians in seeing a cross-Channel invasion in 1942 as being the shortest and most effective route into Germany's heartland and the most appropriate course that the conduct

of the war should take. Their logic was quite simple: first, it was the only place in which a powerful offensive could be quickly organised and executed in the shortest time-scale (other routes would involve longer sea distances); second, air superiority from English bases could be maintained over the bridgehead; and, finally, British and American forces could be launched as a combined effort under combined control.

Britain saw things differently. Convinced that the invasion of mainland Europe, especially France, could only be undertaken when the capability of landing and supplying overwhelming numbers of Allied ground forces was possible, Churchill favoured an alternative strategy. He proposed that the Allies should close a ring around German territories in Europe and the Mediterranean, blocking any further expansion. They should then tighten the blockade of Germany and Italy; give assistance to Russia by all possible means; intensify the RAF bombardment of Germany's manufacturing base with the help of the USAAF; and encourage the spirit of revolt in the people of the occupied countries. In addition, he proposed that the first use of American combat troops should be in support of British operations against the Germans in North Africa.

The Americans were very suspicious

The Supreme Commander, Eisenhower, with Churchill (in the characteristic boiler suit) and Commonwealth Premiers, visit the invasion preparations shortly before D-Day (IWM).

of Churchill's motives with such a strategy, fearing that it concentrated more on Imperial Britain's possible post-war intentions, rather than being the shortest means of ending the war. However, Churchill managed to get his way with Roosevelt, for it had been recognised by the Combined Chiefs of Staff that the lack of appropriate shipping, especially landing craft, would remain a limiting factor governing any cross-Channel attack until mid-1943. An American landing in North Africa would at least enable the early entry of American combat troops into the war and would help to raise morale in the USA. As a result, American troops successfully landed in French North Africa in November 1942 but Roosevelt's advisors were adamant that there were to be no more 'side-shows' or peripheral operations.

What did take place in August 1942 was a combined operations raid in strength on the fortified north French port of Dieppe, in which Southampton played a great part. Most of the ships and troops embarked through the port. The main purpose of the operation was to test the amphibious warfare tactics that had been developed over the preceding two years. Dieppe was chosen as being a good example of the type of port that would have to be captured and held during the main invasion, in order to allow the rapid build-up of forces into the bridgehead. The target was well within range of fighter cover from airfields in southern England and could test the value of air support. The raid also served the purpose of probing the effectiveness of German defences. Finally, as part of an offensive operation, the use of the port was to be denied to the enemy by its complete demolition at the end of the raid.

The attack was not a success. The troops in the main landings were pinned down on the shoreline. Those tanks that were put ashore could not cross the sea wall and floundered on the shingle beach.

Most of the troops that did reach the promenade were destroyed by enemy machine gun fire. On either flank the story was basically the same; beach defences kept the infantry confined to the water's edge. During the operation the Germans lost some 600 men, whilst the Allies lost over 4,000, with one destroyer, 33 landing craft and 109 aircraft destroyed in the raid.

The operation was a great propaganda coup for the Nazis. Pictures of crippled tanks and dead bodies on the beach were exploited as a sign of the invincibility of Hitler's Fortress Europe. Nonetheless, despite what amounted to a disaster, the raid was invaluable for the amount of new information gained from it.

These lessons were put to good use during the planning for the invasion proper. The main points were as follows: first, the 'second front' landings would have to be made over open beaches and not against a fortified port area; second, naval support from heavy guns was essential to eliminate all enemy strong points; third, specialised weapons designed for beach operations would have to be developed to allow armoured support to get off the beach; and, finally, the invasion would have to be a truly combined operation, rather than a series of individual battles fought by the three different services.

The heavy losses suffered during the Dieppe raid clearly demonstrated the strength of German forces along the Channel coast. The comparative ease with which those troops in the area dealt with the attack convinced Hitler that there was no need to divert other divisions from the Russian front to guard against future raids. It had become very clear to the Allies that any return in force to the mainland of Europe would have to be on a scale that was, in 1942, beyond their present capabilities and, as far as Churchill was concerned, probably those of 1943 as well.

It was an argument in which Churchill got his own way, at least during 1943. There was no invasion against northern Europe that year, the Allies continued their activities in the Mediterranean. After Axis forces had been eliminated from North Africa, British and American troops landed in Sicily and then Italy. But, whilst the Americans accepted these 'side-show' operations as being expedient for 1943, they were resolute in their belief that a cross-Channel invasion should take place by May 1944. To this end, in April 1943, Lieutenant General F.E. Morgan was appointed as Chief of Staff to the Supreme Allied Commander (COSSAC) to take charge of the planning of the invasion until the time when a Supreme Commander could be chosen. From this moment, plans for the invasion began to gather pace. The amphibious operation that was to return Allied ground troops to the mainland of continental Europe was given the codename OVERLORD. All of the problems that had been identified from previous raids and operations were studied and possible solutions to them considered. For the first time some scale was put on the size of the operation. There was, however, a limiting element to Morgan's plan in the availability of sufficient numbers of landing craft. The Mediterranean operations required great numbers for the Sicily, Salerno and Anzio attacks, whilst the quantity required for the island-hopping strategy being pursued in the Pacific theatre was almost insatiable. Shipyards in Britain and America were working at full capacity to produce them but supply still fell well short of demand.

The proposed invasion would take place with three seaborne divisions and two airborne brigades in the assault, with two more divisions in the immediate follow up. Although at first glance this might seem an impressive force, it was no larger than the assault group that had landed on Sicily against much weaker opposition. Everyone at COSSAC knew that the weight of attack was too slight, but they continued to work out a viable plan under the constraints placed upon them.

It now remained for a site to be chosen for the landings, although for some time there was consensus that only one area was really suitable: Normandy. There were many limiting factors for an invasion site, the prime one being the radius of air cover, then about 150 miles. Other important elements were: the length of sea crossing; the strength of enemy defences; the availability of suitable beaches and the proximity of port installations. The choice came down to just four areas: the Pas de Calais, Normandy, the Cotentin Peninsula and Brittany.

Some commanders, including the redoubtable General George Patton, favoured the Pas de Calais. It was the shortest sea crossing, well within the range of air cover and provided the quickest route into the heartland of Germany. Unfortunately, it was also the obvious choice and the Germans had ensured that the area had been very heavily fortified. Its defences were quite formidable. Morgan and his staff quickly rejected it as being unsuitable.

Brittany included the large ports of Brest and St Nazaire, had a less well defended coastline and was blessed with good wide beaches, but the region was rejected because of the longer sea route and for being beyond the reach of dominant air cover. The Cotentin, with its port at Cherbourg, was considered but its main problem was the possibility

that the landings could be easily contained on the peninsula by a strong German force across its base. COSSAC was left with Normandy as being the area with an acceptable compromise of all of the limiting factors.

The Normandy coastline was defended, but not to the same extent as that around the Pas de Calais. The sea route was not over-long and could be adequately covered by an air defence screen. It had numbers of open beaches, with good access into the hinterland. And, finally, the ports of Cherbourg and Le Havre were close by. A section of coastline along the Bay of the Seine between the Vire and Orne rivers was therefore chosen as the proposed landing area.

Once the decision to make the landings in Normandy had been taken, Hampshire, situated directly across the Channel from the French province, became the obvious choice as the main concentration area and as the launch pad for the invasion. The county contained Southampton, the largest passenger port in the country, perfect for handling extensive numbers of troops. Its unique four high tides a day gave it a capacity that was unmatched along the south coast of England. A few miles to the east was Portsmouth, the nation's premier naval port and the home of the Royal Navy. Just offshore was the

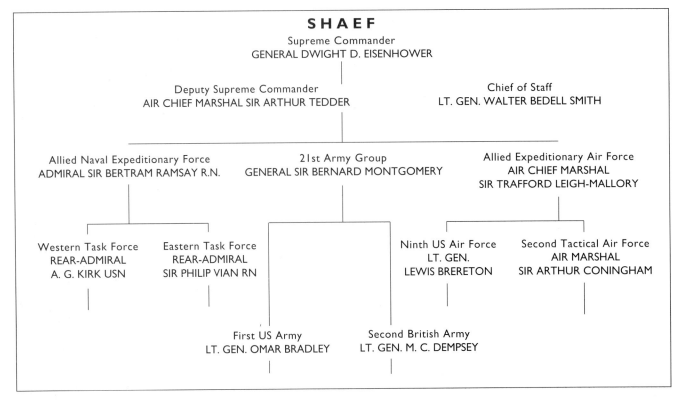

S H A E F
Supreme Commander
GENERAL DWIGHT D. EISENHOWER

Deputy Supreme Commander
AIR CHIEF MARSHAL SIR ARTHUR TEDDER

Chief of Staff
LT. GEN. WALTER BEDELL SMITH

Allied Naval Expeditionary Force
ADMIRAL SIR BERTRAM RAMSAY R.N.

21st Army Group
GENERAL SIR BERNARD MONTGOMERY

Allied Expeditionary Air Force
AIR CHIEF MARSHAL
SIR TRAFFORD LEIGH-MALLORY

Western Task Force
REAR-ADMIRAL
A. G. KIRK USN

Eastern Task Force
REAR-ADMIRAL
SIR PHILIP VIAN RN

Ninth US Air Force
LT. GEN.
LEWIS BRERETON

Second Tactical Air Force
AIR MARSHAL
SIR ARTHUR CONINGHAM

First US Army
LT. GEN. OMAR BRADLEY

Second British Army
LT. GEN. M. C. DEMPSEY

The Allied Command structure for Overlord

sheltered anchorage of the Solent, perfect as a site for the assembly of the invasion fleet. The road and rail network feeding the two ports was suitable for handling the movement of the volumes of men and *matériel* that would be required for the attack and the inlets, creeks and harbours of the Solent could hide a multitude of craft well away from the enemy's prying eyes. Hampshire was well suited for the task of springboard for the Normandy landings.

General Morgan and his COSSAC staff spent the remainder of 1943 at their headquarters in Norfolk House, planning for OVERLORD. The proposed size of the assault force and weight of resources originally allocated were clearly not enough, but political and military necessity dictated that it was all that Morgan could expect. The team were labouring under the handicap of not yet having a Supreme Commander with the appropriate authority to

argue various matters for them.

In December 1943, the Supreme Commander for Operation OVERLORD was appointed. The two most powerful and able soldiers in the American and British armies were considered for the post: General George C. Marshall, US Army Chief of Staff, and General Sir Alan Brooke, Chief of the Imperial General Staff. Both men were ruled out: Marshall because President Roosevelt could not spare him and

Brooke because he was British. With most of the effort in Europe, both on D-Day and in the subsequent push into Germany, being provided by the Americans, it was politic that the Supreme Commander should be from the USA. General Dwight D. Eisenhower was given the job in recognition for his successes in North Africa and the Mediterranean.

The appointees to all three of the subordinate commands for the operation were British: General Sir Bernard Montgomery was to command all of the land forces in 21st Army Group, both British and American, until such times as Eisenhower could take overall command in the field; Admiral Sir Bertram Ramsay was to head the Allied Naval Expeditionary Force and Air Chief Marshal Sir Trafford Leigh-Mallory was appointed to lead the Allied Expeditionary Air Force. The Deputy Supreme Commander, Air Chief Marshal Sir Arthur Tedder, was also British. This team of commanders took over the responsibility for the planning of OVERLORD from COSSAC and worked together as the Supreme Headquarters of the Allied Expeditionary Forces (SHAEF) in London.

By the time that the final team had been appointed, much of the basic preparation for OVERLORD had been completed by COSSAC. Intelligence gathering had quantified

Admiral Ramsay and General Eisenhower at Southwick House (IWM)

the defences and was monitoring any changes the Germans might make to them. Embarkation points had been prepared, concentration areas laid out, logistics systems organised, supplies stockpiled and shipping assigned. These tasks were necessary whatever the size and scope of the battle plan and whoever the command team happened to be. However, the new men at SHAEF, and especially Montgomery and

Eisenhower, were not entirely happy when they saw COSSAC's plan.

Montgomery felt that the attack was on too narrow a front and the subsequent build-up of troops into what could become a very confined area, would lead to confusion and congestion. Eisenhower was unhappy with the planned numbers of troops that were involved in the initial assault. He insisted that the attack should be made with five seaborne and three airborne divisions. Montgomery suggested that the British and American armies should each have their own area of landing beaches and the freedom to enlarge their own section of beachhead as the tactical situation allowed. The two sectors would then meet up and act strategically to capture the two ports of Cherbourg and Le Havre, in order to quicken the build-up of troops into the lodgement area. Eisenhower agreed with the proposed changes and ordered the plan to be modified.

As a consequence of these misgivings, the plan was enlarged to accommodate two extra landing beaches: one in the American sector and one in the British. The final agenda for OVERLORD dictated that the Americans would now land astride the River Vire, with their right-hand attack launched against the beach codenamed UTAH on the base of the Cotentin Peninsula. Their left hand wave would hit the beach called OMAHA located in front of Vierville. The extra beach assigned to the British was SWORD, situated to the west of Ouistreham, near the mouth of the River Orne. Next to this was the area JUNO, opposite Courseulles, with the right-hand side of the British assault landing on sector GOLD, covering the Port-en-Bessin to Arromanches stretch of the Normandy coastline.

The Allied order of battle for the attack was as follows: the First US Army, commanded by Lieutenant General Omar Bradley, would lead the assault with the 4th and 1st US Infantry Divisions landing on UTAH and OMAHA respectively. The Second British Army, commanded by Lieutenant General Miles Dempsey, would use the 50th Northumbrian Division, the 3rd Canadian Infantry Division and the 3rd British Infantry Division to assault GOLD, JUNO and SWORD beaches in that order.

The number of airborne troops allocated to the invasion was also increased. Two American divisions, the US 82nd and 101st Airborne Divisions, were to be dropped to seize vital road junctions and bridges and to seal off the base of the Cotentin Peninsula in order to protect the western extremity of the lodgement area. In the east, the same type of strategic tasks were given to the British 6th Airborne Division.

With the OVERLORD plan having been enlarged to cope with the demands of the new commanders, the original date set for the invasion had to be put back. The intended landings were supposed to take place in May 1944 but these changes dictated that early June would now be the earliest possible date for the attack. Even this would be a very difficult date to meet, for there was still an acute shortage of landing craft. The first week in June was provisionally set as the likely target for D-Day.

The landing beaches stretched across the north Normandy coastline from west to east: UTAH, OMAHA, GOLD, JUNO and SWORD. On the British coast opposite, the embarkation areas allocated for the assembly of the troops and equipment needed to attack those beaches corresponded to the geographical location of the landing sites themselves. The most westerly group, the American troops destined for UTAH, assembled in Devon around Torbay. OMAHA Beach assault force concentrated in Dorset between Poole Harbour and Portland. The British and Canadians landing on GOLD, JUNO and SWORD beaches, assembled in Hampshire and West Sussex. The airborne troops left from airfields in Berkshire and the Midlands, with some glider forces embarking from Dorset.

The OVERLORD plan was to put eight Allied divisions into Normandy in the first few hours of D-Day. Opposing them initially would be four German divisions, with perhaps three more divisions, including two armoured, reaching the area later in the day. The changes made to the plan had added extra weight to the assault and the balance of power clearly lay with the Allies, providing everything went according to plan. The crux of the battle for Normandy would come during the few days after the landings, when the Germans had had time to react and brought their armoured divisions into action against the invaders. The climax would be not so much the seizing of a bridgehead, but holding on to the lodgement area once the enemy began to make determined efforts to throw the Allies back into the sea. It was essential that the build-up of troops over the beaches and into the lodgement area exceeded the enemy's attempts to counter them with a build-up of his own.

As the assault troops for the invasion began sailing from their south coast ports, elsewhere in England other groups would be embarking to join in the battle as part of the second wave. From Southend the 51st (Highland) Division would head for SWORD; from Felixstowe the 49th Division was destined for GOLD, along with the 7th Armoured Division; from Fowey the US 29th Infantry Division was intending to land at OMAHA, together with the US 2nd Infantry Division from Swansea, and UTAH would be the target for the US 9th and 90th Infantry Divisions, sailing from the ports of Bristol and Cardiff. By the end of the second day, the Allies planned to have 13 divisions in the lodgement area, with 17 by D-Day plus 3 and 21 by D-Day plus 12.

The naval plan for OVERLORD was given the codename NEPTUNE.

King George VI and General Montgomery at Monty's Tactical HQ at Broomfield House in the spring of 1944 (IWM)

Admiral Sir Bertram Ramsay had been given command of what was to be the greatest invasion force the world has ever known. Every aspect of the assault was quite staggering; a fleet of almost 7,000 vessels was available to carry out the operation. Of these, over 4,000 were ships and landing craft engaged in the assault and follow-up stages. To protect the fleet and to blast the enemy ashore, 1,200 naval vessels were assigned to the task. In support, 736 ancillary craft and 864 merchant supply ships added their weight to the armada. The invasion fleet was divided into two task forces: Rear-Admiral Sir Philip Vian commanded the Eastern Task Force covering the British sector, whilst the American sector was served by Rear-Admiral A.G. Kirk and his Western Task Force.

The roll of the air forces was equal to those of the other services. Their contribution began long before even the date of the invasion was known. In order to seal off the Normandy area and interfere with enemy troop movements against the invasion coast, all of the bridges over the Seine and Loire rivers were destroyed, along with strategic road and rail networks. This bombing campaign started early in 1944, not only in the Normandy area but all over northern France. It was important to keep the enemy guessing as to where the invasion would land. The air forces went to great lengths to ensure that Normandy did not receive any more strategic bombing than other areas of France, in order to prevent the Germans from assuming too much. Two tactical air forces were assigned to these tasks: the Ninth US Air Force commanded by Lieutenant General Lewis Brereton and the British Second Tactical Air Force under Air Marshal Sir Arthur Coningham.

Nearer to the time of the invasion, the air forces switched their targets to enemy radar installations, beach defences, supply dumps and communications networks. To continue with the deception and to confuse the enemy, for every site within the Normandy area that was bombed, two more were bombed outside the area. For the invasion itself, Air Chief Marshal Leigh-Mallory had 11,500 aircraft at his disposal. Heavy bombers amounted to over 3,400 of these aircraft, with 930 medium bombers completing the offensive arm. Almost 3,800 fighters protected the air and sea armadas and provided ground support to the land forces. 1,360 transport aircraft provided the massive airlift for the three parachute divisions involved in the initial assault, with their heavy equipment and more troops being carried in 3,500 gliders. There were also 500 reconnaissance aircraft watching for enemy movements on land and 1,000 planes from Coastal Command seeking him out at sea.

That was the battle plan; but what of the lessons learned from combined operations and the disastrous Dieppe raid? The difficulties of landing amphibious troops on an enemy-held coastline and the problems of support and resupply were clearly understood by this time. Strong points and beach defences had to be eliminated before the first troops hit the shore. Specialised equipment to deal with localised resistance and beach obstacles needed development. The immediate capture of port facilities to land heavy supplies was essential. Air support for the attack needed to be controlled from the front line, communications networks needed to be set up, repair facilities produced, advanced landing grounds built, and so on. For every problem that was identified, a solution had to be found. Some of these solutions appeared quite fanciful and might have seemed impossible: but they actually worked.

In the same way that geography had made Hampshire the natural choice as the launch pad for the main parts of the D-Day armada, so the county was the obvious location for the production of essential specialised equipment. Hampshire became the arsenal for D-Day and its workers and industries played a crucial role in preparing and supplying Operation OVERLORD. This task was to place unprecedented demands on the county, but these demands were met in full, and beyond, as Hampshire's economy was turned to preparing for the liberation of occupied Europe.

CHAPTER TWO

THE ECONOMIC BASE FOR OVERLORD

Martin Polley

When the decision was made that Normandy was to be the site of the Allied invasion of Europe, it immediately fell to Hampshire to provide the base for the build-up and execution of the attack. The county offered the closest Allied-held land to Normandy and had the geographical advantage of the double high water at Southampton that would enable the number of troop and supply shipments to be twice as high as from other ports on the south coast. Hampshire also possessed various logistical advantages: these included an established rail infrastructure that was part of the Southern Railway's network; the Royal Dockyard at Portsmouth, complete with its facilities for shipbuilding, repairs, victualling and technological development; and the commercial docks at Southampton, with their dry dock facilities. Southampton was chosen as the main embarkation point, maintaining its long history as the 'English Gateway' that had seen it serve this purpose for previous wars in the Crimea, Egypt, southern Africa and Europe,

the latter including the despatch of the unsuccessful BEF (British Expeditionary Force) in 1940. With Southampton as 'the base and sally-port for a great assault', and Portsmouth also critical to the invasion's success, the rest of the county of Hampshire worked behind them to provide the logistical support necessary for the success of the invasion in the areas of supply, storage, and construction.

Between 1942 and the invasion in June 1944, a number of demands on the area's infrastructure were made so that the Allied force would be adequately transported, housed, shipped and supplied. Additionally, the force required the production of a number of essential tools, ranging from landing craft to synthetic harbours, from ammunition to submarine oil pipelines. The logistical contribution made by Hampshire also required labour. The wartime labour market was obviously unusual, as military conscription removed the bulk of the male workforce and their places had to be filled from reserve sources. These included

women, the retired, migrant labour from other parts of the United Kingdom and neutral Ireland, and the unskilled. These personnel were employed in work on the infrastructure in Hampshire and on new industrial projects. In addition to accommodating these people, action had to be taken to regulate the supply of skilled labour in such key sectors of production as iron and steel, mining, and shipbuilding. A study of the labour force working for Hampshire's contribution to OVERLORD provides information about many of these areas of the management of the nation's wartime economy. Hampshire thus provided space, labour and time for the planning of OVERLORD, and its contribution was absolutely vital to the success of the enterprise.

The Ports

The planning of operations OVERLORD and NEPTUNE (the actual assault stage of the invasion) used Southampton as the main port of embarkation. Its geographical

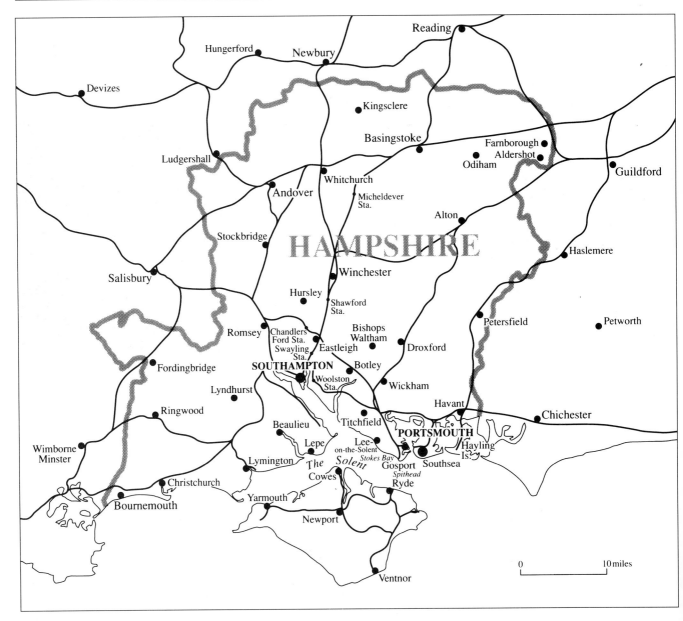

Hampshire in 1943, showing major population centres, rail lines and a selection of places mentioned in the text.

Vehicles for D-Day waiting to embark at the new docks in Southampton (HJC)

advantage of double high water, in which the outgoing high tide from the Needles was forced back at Spithead, made it 'the only port in the British Isles which could be entered at all states of the tide by the largest vessels afloat'. This ensured its development as a primary military port from the late Victorian period and in 1894 it was designated as the country's chief military port. Its importance, however, did not rest solely on its military uses. The commercial developments that it experienced from the end of the nineteenth century were also essential to the planning and execution of OVERLORD. The docks had attracted commercial development from the successive railway companies, London and South West Railway (LSWR) and Southern Railway, and from the ocean liner companies, Cunard and White Star, both of which made Southampton the European base of their transatlantic services. The investment of these companies left Southampton with unique facilities, including, by 1914, two of the world's largest dry docks; and it could claim, besides its distinction as the principal military port, to be the country's 'principal ocean passenger port'. These new

The D-Day build-up: US personnel and tanks in Southampton Docks, 16th August 1943 (ABP Southampton)

developments enabled Southampton to host large-scale military operations in the First World War, when over 8,000,000 troops and 200,000 guns, limbers and other vehicles passed through Southampton on their way to the Continent.

Between the wars, the docks had been extended and their management rationalised. After the 1923 Railways Act, the new Southern Railway Company invested heavily in the building of the Western Docks, including the reclamation of 400 acres and, later, the construction of the King George V Graving Dock, the largest of its kind in the world. These developments were to prove essential to the success of the invasion of Europe in 1944, as they provided an infrastructure that was able to accommodate the necessary invasion fleet as well as the construction of components for the synthetic harbours. In 1939, as in 1914, Southampton could be converted with relative ease to the demands of war. By this time, the city stood, in the words of its proudest historian, 'at the peak of its modern economic fame': the declaration of war in September 1939 was to see it return to 'its traditional avocation' as a military base. The immediate military needs of the period from the outbreak of war to June 1940 saw Southampton handling 71,337 vehicles, 311,352 tons of cargo, and 795,743 troops in outward and inward movements. The port, and a number of its ships, were also to play an important part in Operation DYNAMO, the evacuation of the BEF from Dunkirk. Although the bulk of the evacuation fleet was provided by the Royal Navy, the famous armada of small boats included Southern Railway's cross-Channel ferries *Lorina* and *Normannia*, and Red Funnel's Isle of Wight ferry *Gracie Fields*. The latter was lost, and was eulogised by J.B. Priestley in his famous 'Postscript' broadcast on Dunkirk as one of the 'shilling sicks' that had 'paddled and churned away for ever'.

Southampton was an obvious target for the German air offensive against Great Britain. Between DYNAMO and OVERLORD the docks provided a prime military target to Germany and the city endured heavy bombing and enormous damage to property: the November 1940 blitz, for example, reduced Southampton's rateable value by 12.5%, the third largest decrease in England and Wales outside London. Sporting facilities were also damaged: one German bomb famously landed in the penalty area of The Dell's Milton Road end, breaking a water culvert and flooding the pitch. Football was clearly good for the morale of the town and its people, and the game was easily accommodated elsewhere: but dislocation of the docks would have been far more damaging. This never happened, and the destruction was limited. Alongside physical survival came economic recovery, and by 1942 the docks had gone through the worst of their wartime depression caused by the fall of imports and exports from 1,100,000 freight tons in 1939 to 40,000 in 1941. The economic upturn came with the introduction of the Lend-Lease programme of American imports, and the freight tonnage for 1942 was back up to pre-war levels.

The survival and development of the infrastructure were assured in 1942 by the military decision to use Southampton as the major embarkation port for the invasion of Europe. In July of that year, the Military Movement Control installed itself in the South-Western Hotel; while the following summer, the American Army established the Headquarters 14th Major Port in Southampton. These arrivals heralded a new phase in the city's history: its transformation into what Southampton's biographer has called 'the largest naval and military base that the world had yet seen'. The next two years saw this build-

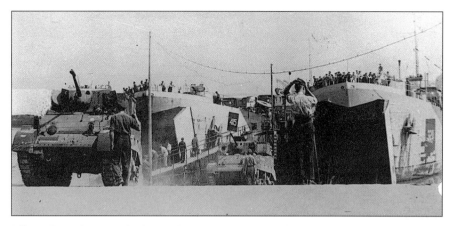

US-made tanks disembark on a hard at Portsmouth (ENHT)

up take place in various forms across south Hampshire, bordered by Sparsholt, Hedge End and Bushfield. For example, Southampton Common became a massive encampment; camouflage turned The Avenue into 'a leafy tunnel impenetrable to eyes above'; and security measures turned residents into permit holders, a restriction shared

US Navy personnel at Portsmouth prepare for D-Day (ENHT)

with civilians living in the whole of a 10-mile-wide coastal strip from Land's End to The Wash. In all, by April 1944, 'the whole Southampton area had become one vast camp, ammunition dump and airfield'.

The early twentieth century had also seen developments in the maritime infrastructure at Portsmouth, most notably the Royal Dockyard's increased capacity to manage larger ships of the Dreadnought class. However, the inter-war slump that missed Southampton thanks to its commercial traffic hit Portsmouth because of its lack of diversity in a period of disarmament: in 1931, for example, only 10,000 men were employed by the Dockyard, whereas 23,000 had been in 1917. As Raymond Riley put it, Portsmouth has historically been 'a hostage to the press of naval activity rather than to the market forces that drive most towns'. This factor ensured a boom for the city thanks to the naval rearmament programme from the mid-1930s, as the Dockyard was used for limited ship-building and larger scale repair and refitting work that were to prove useful for the preparations for D-Day. Portsmouth was the base for the convoy escorts supporting the troops of the BEF in 1939 and 1940, and also contributed a range of vessels to DYNAMO. The city naturally provided a military target for the Luftwaffe, and the Dockyard, like much of the city, suffered extensive damage. This was not fatal, however, and from March 1942 the Dockyard began planning for the berthing and supply of the naval force for the invasion. It also hosted experiments

Landing craft in dry-dock in Southampton (HJC)

on the breakwaters for the artificial harbours, and, like Southampton, provided accommodation for the construction of some of the components for MULBERRY.

The county's maritime infrastructure, based around Southampton and Portsmouth, was called upon to play various parts in the preparations and launching of the invasion. The basic one was the provision of berthing accommodation for the vessels that made up the invasion fleet, estimated at around 7,000 in all.

In addition to mooring requirements, space was needed to maintain the essential programmes of shipbuilding and repair, to unload the Lend-Lease imports and handle the ships bringing servicemen from the United States to Great Britain as part of

The Empress Dock, Southampton, in the last stages of preparations for D-Day (HJC)

Churchill tanks practise landing from an LST at Beach Street hard, Portsmouth (ENHT)

Operation BOLERO, and to construct and assemble the various components for MULBERRY. The Southampton docks manager, quoted by Knowles, illustrates the problem:

"The Navy wanted accommodation for craft of all sizes for laying up and repair; the Army had to be satisfied as to berths for the troops to embark, and room for their mechanical transport, equipment and stores; hospital ships, and ships with fresh water for the 'operation' had to be accommodated…It was also to be borne in mind that eventually the United States Army authorities would want room to ship their troops and equipment; and with all this, the commercial programme had to be maintained and stopped only when operational needs made that course compulsory."

The scale of the task can also be illustrated by the contemporary observation, only slightly exaggerated, that in the days before D-Day one could walk dryshod from the mainland to the Isle of Wight from vessel to vessel.

The main docks were clearly going to be too small for this task, even allowing for the inter-war reclamation programme at Southampton, and a variety of expedient measures were introduced to provide berthing of suitable depths and convenient distances. This included the exploitation of natural features, such as mooring shallow craft in the Beaulieu river and at Calshot, as well as hastily erecting new man-made berths, such as the piles

placed in the Itchen below Northam Bridge. As the build-up continued, emergency berthing procedures had to be followed, such as mooring vessels eight abreast. The vessels thus berthed were fed and watered by the small fleet from the Royal Clarence Yard at Portsmouth, providing a daily supply of 20,000 tons of fresh water and 33,000 pounds of bread, and weekly supplies of 400 tons of potatoes, 100 tons of meat and 50 tons of fresh vegetables. As well as berthing facilities, the docks had to provide sufficient facilities for embarkation of troops and loading of supplies. As the NEPTUNE plans required that the landing craft be able to empty their contents either on to open beaches or on to pier-heads in the artificial harbours, a system of slipways and ramps was required for the embarkation and loading process. In this way, the craft could be loaded without having to run aground, a time-consuming and potentially dangerous process. Existing commercial slipways were called into use throughout the Southampton and Portsmouth area, such as those of Thornycroft at Woolston and Moody at Bursledon. In addition, approximately 130 new concrete and steel hards were built on beaches and in the ports to accommodate the fleet of landing craft.

Another essential supply requirement of the invading force was petroleum, oil and lubricants (POL), and there were logistical problems in relying solely on transportation by ship, notably the high demand and the unloading requirements of tankers. The problem was solved by what Knowles has called a scheme that 'ranked second in its audacity only to the MULBERRY project itself': the system of submarine pipelines known as PLUTO (generally said to stand for 'Pipeline Under the Ocean', although the Public Record Office shelf list labels it as 'Pipeline Underwater Transport of Oil'). Using this method of supply, oil could be pumped directly from the south coast to the far shore, thus incurring none of the risks or capacity problems of using shipping. A flexible pipeline system, laid underwater from rolling drums, was developed from 1942, with tests in the Thames and the Bristol Channel establishing a fast system of laying. In 1943 the Southampton area became crucially involved in the PLUTO operation in two ways. First, the Shell-Mex/BP oil storage plant at Hamble was selected as the supply base for the project. Accordingly, an extended jetty was constructed so that additional numbers of craft could be moored for simultaneous loading. Second, the Admiralty requisitioned the remains of the bombed Supermarine Spitfire factory at Woolston, naming it H.M.S. *Abatos* and basing their planning team for PLUTO there. Pumping

One of the PLUTO 'Conums' at Sandown, Isle of Wight (IWM)

stations were built at Sandown on the Isle of Wight to feed Cherbourg with four pipes, and at Dungeness in Kent to feed Boulogne with 16 pipes. Using ships to transport the oil from Hamble to Lepe (where it was piped to the Isle of Wight) and to Dungeness, some 2,000,000 tons of POL were supplied by Hamble between D-Day and VE-Day, providing an hourly supply of approximately 600 tons at the beachheads. This innovative method of supply worked extremely well, ensuring adequate fuel supplies for the invading force's vehicles and their needs for lubricants, and its scale caused General Dwight Eisenhower's naval aide Captain Harry Butcher to remark in his diary on 29th May 1944 that it would 'in itself be regarded as a considerable enterprise in normal times'.

For all these aspects of the ports' work to succeed, more than just accommodation and facilities were needed, and the role of the labour force in the success of the operation cannot be neglected. The whole of OVERLORD relied heavily on skilled labourers at key points around the country, augmented by conscripted unskilled labour, and this obviously placed strains on personnel resources that were seen in various sectors: for example, the MULBERRY project diverted scaffolders from building work. Similar strains were also felt in the docks and the shipyards as D-Day approached, and various projects were initiated to fill the gaps.

As in previous boom times, the British government turned to the labour market of Eire and Northern Ireland to fill some of the gaps left by military service, and Hampshire

Dockers discharge US tanks at Southampton, 16th August 1943 (ABP Southampton)

was to accommodate a small proportion of this workforce. In shipbuilding and ship repairing, for example, the Ministry of Labour and National Service started a recruitment programme in 1942 that was to bring some Irishmen into Hampshire. The Ministry's Southern Regional Office at Reading asked firms in the area for their requirements, and requests for a total of 119 men were received from the Southampton sites of Thornycroft, Southern Railway, Harland and Wolff, and Risdon Beazley. These were sent to the Ministry with the optimistic note from the Regional Office that a 'good type of male labour' could be supplied from Northern Ireland: 'the poor standard of unskilled men we have been compelled to put into the Shipyards is a cause of frequent complaint.' However, the demands from the Scottish region were greater, and the bulk was accommodated there. Thornycroft received only 32 Irish workers up to the end of 1943. There were, of course, security reasons that made the Government and the contractors wary of employing Irishmen, and workers from Northern Ireland were explicitly preferred to men from neutral Eire. There were also some social problems between the few Irish who worked in Hampshire and the local populations. This had been foreseen by the Admiralty in September 1943, when the Ministry of Labour and National Service's regional offices were circularised on the need to smooth over the 'serious difficulties' that arose because of 'Local [sic] prejudice amongst householders against accepting Irish labour in lodgings and billets'.

Another sector of the essential dock work that was to come under heavy strain during the military operations of OVERLORD was loading and bunkering. In September 1943, the responsible government departments estimated that 30,000 tons of supplies would need to be loaded through the country's eleven main docks, including Southampton and Portsmouth. In February 1943, the Ministry of War Transport and the National Dock Labour Corporation (NDLC) began working on the problem of 'additional labour requirements for port working which may arise should certain operations take place': the guarded language of the period is interesting and characterises a great deal of the official documentation in the planning stages. The Ministry and the NDLC met to discuss solutions, and came up at first with the idea of combing the Dormant Register for suitable men. But local research proved this to be a worthless exercise: in Southampton, where an estimated

2,500 extra workers were needed, the register listed only 553, many of whom were already employed in priority work, such as aircraft production. The shipbuilding industry was also ruled out as a possible major contributor, with only an estimated 250 men available from that sector. In the words of the informant:

> "The circumstances which may increase our need for dockers will I think also increase the urgency of ship repair work and it is unlikely that we should get many from that industry."

In the light of these problems of recruitment, the NDLC and Ministry of War Transport next turned to the idea of Dockers' Flying Squads, mobile units made up of conscripted men who would be given a month's training in dock work, then relegated to the reserve with military rank until they were required for operational purposes. The Ministry of War Transport's Port and Transit Control rejected this scheme in September 1943, arguing that civilians would not quickly integrate with their new place of work and would not be reliable in case of air attack. It was feared that, in the event of an air raid, many would simply leave the job and return home: the lessons of the phenomenon of mass trekking from the blitz period and the disruption it had caused to production had clearly

The build-up continues (ABP Southampton)

been learnt in Whitehall. The problem of accommodation was also highlighted, particularly as it affected south Hampshire, where 1,000 men would need to be housed:

> "Billeting and feeding arrangements for large numbers of transferees would present formidable difficulties at the South Coast ports, and particularly Southampton."

Instead, the armed forces were called upon to provide the labour. The advantages were clear: they could be trusted to be reliable under attack; and the War Office could accommodate them in their own camps. Accordingly, the Ministry of Labour and National Service requested the American army to provide 1,720 men, 1,200 of whom were for Southampton, while the British army was to contribute 330, 100 of whom were for Portsmouth. These figures, projected in September 1943, proved to be too low and the totals grew between then and D-Day. In May 1944, the final allocations were made to fill in the deficiencies: this involved 320 British troops at Portsmouth and 800 at Southampton, while the Americans provided 1,800 for Southampton. Split between bunkering and loading duties, the combined civilian and military dock force helped to maintain the momentum of the operation and their reliability was praised on 8th June 1944 by an official of the NDLC in a letter to the Ministry of Labour and National Service. Referring to the work done at Southampton, he noted that, 'Some gangs who had already worked 24 consecutive hours agreed to continue for another full shift in order to complete the job'. His overall opinion was that, 'The men have responded admirably'.

Hampshire's major ports thus played an essential part in OVERLORD, both in the build-up and the assault phase. Their hinterlands were employed for the accommodation of the force; their docks for the build-up of the naval vessels and for the actual launching of the attack on 6th June 1944. Their role did not stop then. Troops continued to pass through the ports, while servicemen on leave, the wounded, and prisoners of war made the reverse journey. Supplies similarly carried on being passed through, such as the 107 million gallons of fresh water in oil tankers between June 1944 and April 1945. These men and supplies maintained the western Allies in their progress across France and the Low Countries and into Germany. But the docks were not the only part of the county's infrastructure to be over-employed: in order to get the men and supplies to and from Southampton and Portsmouth, the Hampshire section

of the Southern Railway played as important a part.

The Southern Railway in Hampshire

In his history of the Southern Railway during the Second World War, Bernard Darwin describes the railway's involvement in the build-up for OVERLORD as if seen by 'an observer from another planet': the mushrooming of new sidings; the growth of stores and ammunition dumps in the New Forest; and the convergence on the county of 'the tarpaulin armada' of trains carrying supplies for the largest invasion force ever assembled. This imaginative picture helps to establish the size of the task performed by the Southern Railway in Hampshire in moving troops and equipment: and it was a task performed in the face of serious logistical and practical problems.

By 1942, when the planning for the invasion of Europe began, the four rail companies (Southern Railway, Great Western (GWR), London Midland and Scottish (LMS) London and North East (LNE)) were running their operations on a reduced level, thanks to the toll of bomb damage and the difficulty of replacing stock and locomotives. From the outbreak of war to the end of 1941, for example, only 359 new engines were obtained by the

railway companies, whereas the pre-war total for a similar period would have been 1,400. This problem was partially mitigated by the maintenance of stock that would have previously been scrapped – the principle of 'make do and mend' applied on a massive scale – but the problems were large. For example, operating stock (locomotives, passenger-carrying vehicles, trucks and wagons, including privately owned stock) in 1939 totalled 1,331,800; the figure for 1943 was 1,354,100, an increase of only 1.6%. In the same period, passenger traffic had risen from 1,225,500,000 journeys in 1939 to 1,334,600,000 in 1943, an 8.1% increase; and goods traffic had increased by 4.1%, from 288,300,000 in 1939 to 300,800,000 in 1943. These increases in traffic came from various sources. Passenger traffic was boosted by evacuation, family visits, service personnel travelling on leave, and the increasing necessity of living at a distance from work in many cities; while goods traffic was inflated by the rise in imports under Lend-Lease. Both passenger and goods sectors also benefited from fuel rationing that placed restrictions on road use and sent the number of licensed goods vehicles from 492,000 in 1939 to 452,000 in 1943, a drop of 8%. The number of private cars plummeted in the same period from 2,034,000 to 718,000, a drop of 65%. So even without the build-up for the invasion of Europe, the unintegrated railway system was working under increasingly heavy demands. The stresses added by OVERLORD came in the shape of the movement of troops and stores. As the company responsible for linking the bulk of the OVERLORD sites and for conveying the troops on the last stage of their journeys to the ports, Southern Railway had to take a great share of this pressure.

Southern had been established by the Railways Act of 1921, and covered the bulk of the area south of London, Basingstoke, Salisbury and Exeter, with incursions into north Devon and Cornwall, and including the Isle of Wight, a total of approximately 2,200 route miles. As such, Hampshire was only a part of Southern's operations but the location of so many key OVER-LORD sites in Hampshire ensured that it was a part that was to remain in constant action throughout the period. Two principal areas should be assessed in this study: firstly, the volume of trains using Southern during the planning and execution of OVERLORD; and secondly, the physical development of the infrastructure so that it could 'bear the burdens of a military base preparing for a major assault', as official historians Gowing and Hancock have put it. Taken together, these two areas of usage and development

offer an insight into what the company's war historian called 'a vast, complex and triumphant piece of organisation'.

In early November 1942, the wartime co-ordinating agency, the Railway Executive Committee (REC), began to collect particulars from the

The railways' contribution to the war effort (HC, 15/4/44)

four companies of the number of special trains they ran for the government to transport personnel and stores for the fighting services. This practice continued throughout the war, with the companies filling in weekly returns. It became more detailed as the war progressed: to begin with, only the number of trains each company ran, and how many of them originated with that company, were logged; from February 1944, new forms allowed for the breakdown of the statistics into internal personnel moves, personnel from ports, personnel to ports, and stores. It is from these figures that the scale of the Southern Railway's involvement can be seen.

The statistics in themselves are impressive (see Table 1). Between November 1942, when the recording began, until six weeks after D-Day, Southern Railway handled a total of 31,136 special trains, of which 19,001 originated with the company. This averaged out at 1,415 per four-week period. The weekly and monthly totals varied in response to demands and did not go up in a constant rise: however, after the middle of August 1943, there were never less than 1,100 per month and in the week of D-Day itself Southern handled 778 special trains. Of these, 436 were internal personnel movements (56%), 319 were stores movements (41%), and the remaining 23 comprised of moving personnel to and from ports (3%). It was these figures that the General Manager's office sent to Sir Alan Anderson, the Chairman of the REC, under the observation that the figures represented 'a record for us since Dunkirk'. These statistics can be seen as all the more exceptional when they are taken as a proportion of the total number of government specials throughout the routes of the four railway companies. Between them, the four companies owned approximately 20,000 route miles (20,302 at the Railways Act of 1923, with 19,863 handed over to the Government on the occasion of nationalisation in January 1948). Of these, Southern accounted for only 2,200, little over 10%. Yet in the build-up to OVERLORD, Southern handled a far higher proportion of the traffic than this mileage reflected: for example, in the six months before D-Day, Southern handled 18.7% of the total number of government specials (12,167 out of 65,059: see Table 2). The figures, of which these are only a selection, thus show the volume of rail traffic being handled by Southern Railway in the planning of OVERLORD.

Increases in traffic such as this required new work on the infrastructure, in the shape of tracks, sheds, platforms, and sidings. Hampshire gained many of these. In June 1943, for example, Southern

Week ending –	Week ending	No. of trains	Originating
08.11.42 –	28.11.42	721	—
05.12.42 –	26.12.42	864	—
02.01.43 –	23.01.43	727	—
30.01.43 –	20.02.43	655	—
27.02.43 –	20.03.43	790	512
27.03.43 –	17.04.43	767	579
24.04.43 –	15.05.43	720	568
22.05.43 –	12.06.43	866	652
19.06.43 –	10.07.43	830	640
17.07.43 –	07.08.43	876	672
14.08.43 –	04.09.43	1,155	791
11.09.43 –	02.10.43	1,167	834
09.10.43 –	30.10.43	1,850	1,334
06.11.43 –	27.11.43	1,718	1,272
04.12.43 –	25.12.43	1,628	1,243
01.01.44 –	22.01.44	1,484	1,126
29.01.44 –	19.02.44	1,602	1,170
26.02.44 –	18.03.44	1,804	1,226
25.03.44 –	15.04.44	2,187	1,310
22.04.44 –	13.05.44	2,698	1,583
20.05.44 –	10.06.44	2,392	1,429
17.06.44 –	08.07.44	3,635	2,060
Total		31,136	19,001

Table 1: Trains running on Southern Railway for Government purposes, November 1942 – July 1944

Week ending –	Week ending	SR No.	Total No. (GW, LMS, LNER, SR)	SR as %age of total
01.01.44 –	22.01.44	1,484	8,716	17.0%
29.01.44 –	19.02.44	1,602	9,236	17.3%
26.02.44 –	18.03.44	1,804	10,230	17.6%
25.03.44 –	15.04.44	2,187	11,012	19.8%
22.04.44 –	13.05.44	2,698	12,783	21.1%
20.05.44 –	10.06.44	2,392	13,082	18.2%
Total		12,167	65,059	18.7%

Table 2: Southern Railway's government specials as a proportion of the total number.

Railway requested the REC to finance a number of additional works throughout the Eastleigh area 'in connection with certain special stores traffics, for which we have been asked by the Military Authorities'. These included a reception road and four sidings at Micheldever, a 460 ft long platform extension at Botley, a down-and-up loop for 70 wagons at Romsey, and six new sidings at Brockenhurst to relieve the pressure on Eastleigh. Costs varied, with the work at Micheldever estimated at £43,938, but it met with immediate authorisation from the REC and approval by the Treasury. This kind of request for special works was to recur over the course of the year. Millbrook, Fareham, Havant, Southampton, Chandlers Ford and Nursling were among the stations and yards to undergo development to meet the demands of the military build-up in Hampshire. Micheldever has often been singled out for particular praise in this context, with its service of the Ordnance Emergency Depot earning it the label 'the Woolworth depot' thanks to its ability to provide anything that could possibly be required by the military, 'from a nut', as Bernard Darwin put it, 'to the engine for a tank'. The depth of the cuttings at Micheldever, still in use, also served to provide security to the neighbourhood in case of any ordnance accidents or

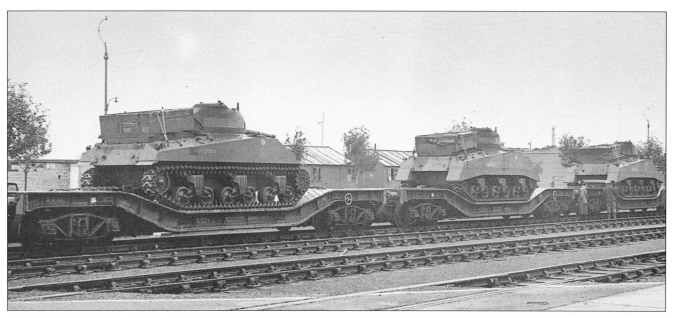

Sherman tanks on transporters, 21st July 1943 (ABP Southampton)

bomb damage. In the words of the company's chairman, work costing 'nearly £1,000,000' was carried out for the special operational requirements of OVERLORD.

As well as development of the actual rail network, special works also covered the building of storage facilities, as exemplified by the hasty search for a suitable site for storing 5,000 tons of bagged coal 'in connection with operational matters' which Southern performed for the Ministry of War Transport in late March 1944: Bevois Park siding was selected. Works such as these on the infrastructure of Hampshire's railways were essential to provide

storage accommodation and rapid loading facilities for the troops and stores that were to pass through the ports. The four railway companies provided 'the conduit pipes to the ports': the geographical location and strategic importance of Hampshire ensured that the Southern Railway, and its staff in Hampshire, had to embrace an inordinate amount of responsibility for the smooth operation of these pipes. Southern Railway, and the stations and staff of the company in Hampshire, thus played a crucial role in moving the necessary troops and stores from all over the country to the embarkation points.

Hampshire's infrastructure of ports

and railways thus made a major contribution to the success of D-Day and to the overall triumph of OVER-LORD. They ensured that men and material were moved and embarked according to plan and that once the beachhead had been established it was fed with adequate supplies to maintain the momentum of the attack, which famously over-stretched itself in the first few days. The dock towns and surrounding areas played a part, too, in accom-modating the Allied force as it built up, filling common land, country-side and residential streets with all kinds of vehicles, weapons and amphibious vessels, ranging from

The Arromanches MULBERRY in operation (by kind permission of the Council of the Institute of Structural Engineers)

Southampton Common hosting a military camp to the newly completed Winchester by-pass becoming a tank park. The Southampton and Portsmouth areas contributed logistically by being turned into the primary supply point of the force; and co-ordinated efforts by the civil and military agencies ensured the smooth operation of the invasion. But the logistical contribution was not limited only to Hampshire's infrastructure. The county's industries were also vital to the success of D-Day.

Industrial Contribution

The role played by various Hampshire firms in building components for the synthetic harbours codenamed MULBERRY was Hampshire's chief industrial contribution to OVERLORD: they provided the bulk of the special sites, the new labour and the round-the-clock building schedules. However, it was not the only industrial or engineering contribution, and firms and sites made other important contributions to the success of OVERLORD. For example, 20,000 tons of ammunition for the Allied forces were manufactured at the Royal Navy's Armaments Depot at Priddy's Hard by an all-female labour force of 1,700. Armaments were also made at Shoreham, Exbury and Marchwood, while Southern Railway's works at

Eastleigh had to cope with diversification. In common with the company's other main works at Brighton, Lancing and Ashford, Eastleigh developed munitions manufacturing alongside its essential railway work. Gun barrels were built in the locomotive works and the paint shop; landing craft and parts for tanks in the machine shop; parts for gliders in the carriage works' paint shop. Other items built or partially built at Eastleigh included scissors bridge layers, gun mountings, motor boats, pontoons and bomb trolleys for 8,000-pounders. Normal carriage and locomotive work continued alongside this military programme and some specialist train conversion was carried out for the needs of the invasion, such as the conversion of carriages, luggage vans and brake vans into ambulance and casualty evacuation stock. By concentrating on the audacious special industrial contribution of the MULBERRY programme, it is easy to neglect such work as this. However, the scale and size of the construction of the synthetic harbours ensure that its importance cannot be underestimated.

MULBERRY Harbours

One of the essential features of the Normandy invasion was the construction and use of the two MULBERRY harbours that were towed across to the landing beaches

and employed for the disembarkation of troops and stores. Historians have argued over the value of these harbours, whose remains at Arromanches have been described as 'a family of elephants taking a bath'. The failure of one of the harbours, for example, is pointed to as evidence of the weakness of the scheme. But the harbours provided the tactical advantage of surprise as well as the logistical advantage of unloading and disembarkation facilities that represented, in the words of scientific historian Guy Hartcup, an imaginative 'use of technology to overcome the disadvantages of landing on a defended shore at the mercy of the weather'.

By late 1942, the need for artificial harbours was accepted as necessary for the success of any assault on Europe. The difficulties of attacking an enemy-held port in order to establish a beachhead had been shown up by the Dieppe raid of August 1942, so anchorage and unloading facilities were required until such time as a suitable French port could be captured and made serviceable after German damage. It was not expected to capture Cherbourg until D-Day plus 40. In the words of a COSSAC letter to 21st Army Group of 21st September 1943:

"The primary object of the artificial harbours is to provide facilities, not subject to interruption by weather, for discharging the minimum maintenance requirements of the force, until such time as the capacities of existing FRENCH ports are able to compete with this requirement."

The plan was not totally original: in his earlier post as First Lord of the Admiralty during the First World War, British Prime Minister Winston Churchill had proposed the construction of artificial harbours in the Heligoland Bight; and the use of blockships had a long history, although their previous usage had tended to be obstructive rather than protective. But the scale of MULBERRY was audacious and was met with scepticism from a number of early planners faced with the proposal that the Allies could take their own harbours with them. General Eisenhower discussed it in his memoirs as a 'project so unique as to be classed by many scoffers as completely fantastic', and recalled his first encounter with the scheme:

"The first time I heard this idea tentatively advanced was by Admiral Mountbatten, in the spring of 1942. At a conference attended by a number of service chiefs he remarked: 'If ports are not available, we may have to construct them in pieces and tow them in.' Hoots and jeers greeted his suggestion but two years later it was to become reality."

The idea was developed at the Largs Combined Operations conference of 28th June 1943, and then finally accepted as a requirement of the invasion at the Quebec conference on 15th August 1943. In the event, two artificial harbours were established: one in the American sector at St Laurent (MULBERRY A), and the more successful one at Arromanches for the British and the Canadians (MULBERRY B). In his memoirs, Churchill labelled them a 'principal part of the great plan', and they were to prove decisive in the rapid unloading of troops and stores in the first days of the invasion, allowing landing craft to unload without grounding and thus turn around regardless of tidal conditions.

The planning for the design and construction of this massive project fell to the British, with American co-operation, and the departmental responsibility was shared between the Admiralty and the War Office with collaboration from the Ministry of Supply. By the end of December 1943 the tough demands to be placed on the synthetic harbours were codified: that they would offer sheltered water for the unloading of 3,000 tons of stores per day by D-Day plus 4; that they would be fully operational by D-Day plus 14, taking 12,000 tons of stores and 1,250 vehicles each day; that they would last for at least 90 days, having withstood 100 mile tows in winds of up to Force 4; and that

their erection would not interfere with the landings. And when the desired capacity of each harbour is taken into account, it becomes clear that Churchill's subsequent description of MULBERRY as constituting 'a multiple problem' was no exaggeration: the harbours had to be able to accommodate 11 Liberty ships 450 ft long and 25 ft deep; up to 40 coasters of 320 ft length and 17 ft depth at any one time, as well 200 tugs and ferries, and room for 1,000 small craft to shelter in bad weather: and all this to be able to continue with up to three sunken ships in the harbour. The harbours also had their own defence requirements, with AA guns and storage for ammunition, oil, and water, and accommodation for up to 500 officers and men. The task has been likened to building two mobile harbours the size of Dover, with the additional problem of the pieces having to be assembled under battle conditions.

Each harbour had a number of components, described by Postan as being 'highly heterogeneous in conception and construction', going by a variety of codenames. It was in their development, construction and assembly that a number of Hampshire locations were to play an important part. The sheltered water was to be guaranteed by a breakwater system. Experiments were conducted on sunken pipes that emitted walls of bubbles and on

Building the MULBERRY harbours: a composite pier being built at Stokes Bay, Hampshire (IWM)

giant plastic balloons anchored by concrete blocks. The Admiralty Experimental Laboratory at Haslar carried out experiments on prototype inflatable rubber versions in Portsmouth Dockyard, described by one of the city's maritime historians as proving 'not surprisingly... to be vulnerable to shrapnel'. In the end, shelter was provided by two sources. First, outer breakwaters were made of blockships, requiring 55 obsolete ships codenamed CORNCOBS to be sunk in position, forming basic harbours codenamed GOOSEBERRY. These provided wide areas of sheltered water for

mooring. The second source, which made up the actual edges of the two MULBERRY harbours, came from inner breakwaters made of two types of specially constructed units: partially submerged steel breakwaters in cruciform, 200 ft long and 25 ft high and weighing 1,000 tons each, codenamed BOMBARDONS; and fully submerged breakwaters made up of cement caissons, codenamed PHOENIXES. The largest of the PHOENIXES weighed in at a displacement of 60,447 tons with a height of 60 ft, a length of 204 ft, and a breadth of 56 ft 3 ins, and they have been described by Cornelius

Ryan as resembling 'a five-storey block of flats lying on its side'. Within the sheltered water thus provided were the landing stages of the harbours, consisting of pontoon pierheads codenamed WHALE and pontoon-based roadways codenamed BEETLE. The pierheads were designed to 'float up & down with the tide', in Churchill's 'celebrated minute' on the problem of landing troops and equipment dryshod. The whole complex was a triumph of expedient engineering and construction, 'a tremendous undertaking' in Churchill's words. The scale of this undertaking can be appreciated further when the time-scale is observed. The idea of synthetic harbours was only fully accepted as an integral part of the invasion plan in August 1943, and the War Office was instructed to build the harbours on 6th September: this provided just nine months to design, commission, construct and assemble the harbours.

Some of the components for the scheme were already in existence, notably the British, French and American vessels to be used as blockships for GOOSEBERRY, although their sacrifice required negotiation: Rear-Admiral William Tennant, who was to co-ordinate the towing of the components and the operation of the harbours, is credited with saying after one fruitless meeting with the Admiralty, 'We came here to get a gooseberry and all we seem to have got is a raspberry'. But the bulk of the components needed to be specially designed and built. The major construction task was the building of the 146 PHOENIX caissons originally ordered. For security reasons, labourers working on the project were not informed of the purpose of the caissons. Angus Calder has written of the rumours spreading that they were 'supporters for colossal nets to trap submarines'. The claim of ignorance is substantiated by oral records of some of the labourers on the Portsmouth and Southampton building projects. They were built in dry docks and on slipways and beaches at various points along the English coastline, with London (East India Dock, Port of London Authority Basin, Surrey Dock, Russia Dock and Woolwich Dock), the Thames Estuary (Grays Basin, Tilbury, Erith, Barking Creek, Barking East Basin), Goole, Tees (Middlesborough), and Bromborough all contributing along with Hampshire.

Hampshire accounted for roughly a third of the completed orders and the total personnel used on the PHOENIX project (see Table 3). The work was contracted out between Pauling, Cochrane and Lovatt at Southampton, and Laing, Lind, Holloway, French, Bovis and Trevor Construction at Portsmouth. The project exploited dry docks, as at Portsmouth and Southampton,

Preparing the beach at Stokes Bay for PHOENIX construction (IWM)

A PHOENIX at Stokes Bay (IWM)

A derelict PHOENIX breakwater beached in Langstone Harbour (PCS)

A section of a composite pier at Stokes Bay (IWM)

along with beach sites, where construction sites and special launching slipways were built for the work, as at Gosport, Lepe and Hayling Island. Each type of site came with its own advantages and drawbacks. In the dry docks of Portsmouth and Southampton, the existing facilities ensured that a full infrastructure of support already existed, such as power generators for floodlighting the round-the-clock work, storage facilities for the steel and concrete needed and canteens for the new labour force. They also offered space: the C-Lock at Portsmouth, for example, accommodated four PHOENIXES at a time, two for Bovis and two for Laing. When each caisson was complete, the dock was simply flooded and they were floated out. This stage of the operation took place under security restrictions to maintain the secrecy of the project from the labourers: men were given a day off on full pay and the work was done by the Navy. The dry docks also offered some protection from the weather to the labourers for a sizeable proportion of the construction process, although as soon as the caisson's height passed the top of the dock, they had to face the elements. Of this process, one labourer recalled, 'They looked after you,…'cos they want you to work through the night, so they supplied duffel coats'. Oilskins were issued in wet weather. However, the drawback for the dock sites was that they offered a known target for any enemy action, and any air raid warnings had to be taken seriously: Lord Haw-Haw had broadcast on the building project, threatening to sink the caissons before they left the English coast. The resultant blackouts evidently caused a number of accidents, some of them fatal, when men fell from scaffolding in the darkness. The three beach sites – Stone Point, Lepe; Stokes Bay, Gosport; and Hayling Island – were not so susceptible to this kind of problem. But they required the construction of special sites for building the caissons and launching them sideways at high tide.

While the PHOENIX programme was Hampshire's main contribution to the construction of MULBERRY components, it was not the only one. BOMBARDON breakwaters and legs for the floating piers were built in Portsmouth and Southampton; and parts for the pierheads and floating roadways were built in Southsea and in specially excavated basins at Beaulieu. Marchwood hosted the assembly point and concreting area for the floats that were to carry the roadways from the pierheads to the beaches. An important design and construction contribution also came from the Gosport yacht building firm of Camper and Nicholson, which developed the

Location	Contractor	Type of Accomodation	No. Ordered	Labour required
Langston Harbour	Trevor	Slipway	4	600
North Point	Lovatt	Slipway	6	700
Portsmouth	Bovis	C Lock	6	460
Portsmouth	Laing	C Lock	6	400
Portsmouth	Lind	Floating Dock	8	700
Southampton No. 5	Paulings	Graving	9	700
Stokes Bay	Holloway	Slipway	8	800
Stokes Bay	French	Slipway	6	600
Hampshire Total			53	4,960
London & Thames			71	7,790
North East			19	1,300
North West			3	450
Total			146	14,500
Hampshire locations as %age of total			36	34

Table 3: The construction of PHOENIX caissons November 1943 – April 1944

SLUG craft (Surf Landing Under Girder). This two-man, twin-engined craft enabled mooring cables to be passed underneath the floating MULBERRY components, linking them to each other.

The personnel for the MULBERRY project across the country as a whole was made up, at a peak, of 45,000 men, many of whom were encouraged into the project by the provision of accommodation and high basic rates of pay as well as the certainty of overtime on a round-the-clock exercise. The labour force at the Hampshire sites came from a variety of sources. Skilled workers, such as scaffolders, steel benders and steel erectors were brought in with the contractors: the steel work on the Bovis

contract at Portsmouth, for example, was carried out by a Liverpool firm, Ron Rivers, who brought their own men. Many of the labourers were men past military age and they were supplemented by younger men conscripted as Bevin Boys into the mining industry and then diverted to MULBERRY. At each site, the workforce was split into teams under individual tradesmen, always under the watchful eye of the civil engineer in charge of the site, and a certain degree of mobility existed between the work forces at different sites: for example, when the work at Portsmouth was complete, a number of the Bovis labourers were moved to Southampton docks to help finish the job there. There is evidence of some friction between labourers and

Above: MULBERRY in action: one of the floating roadways, with numerous SLUG boats in the foreground (IWM)

Opposite: MULBERRY A with US personnel at St Laurent. Note the steel mattresses used to improve the beach surface rolled up in the left foreground (IWM)

the host communities, best exemplified by the complaints from Cadland House to the contractors Wilson Lovatt about the men from the MULBERRY site at Lepe stealing chickens and poaching on the estate.

The failure of MULBERRY A in the storms of June 1944 has often tended to dampen enthusiasm for the whole project. Designed to last for 90 days, storm damage made it virtually unusable by D-Day plus 15, 21st June. But MULBERRY B at Arromanches served its original purpose well and the volume of troops and supplies discharged

through the synthetic harbour was of inestimable value. The whole scheme had come as a surprise to Germany's military planners, who worked on the assumption that the Allies' unloading requirements would gear their attack elsewhere than the open beaches of Normandy. Albert Speer, Germany's Armaments and War Production Minister, reflected on MULBERRY after his release from Spandau as the 'single brilliant technical device' that gave the Allied invasion the advantage over the German defence of France. The whole scheme, in Lesley Burton's words, 'left the enemy gasping on the ropes'. And regardless of its debated worth, the task of designing and constructing MULBERRY was a massive one, undertaken at short notice. As with the infrastructure, it must be remembered that the construction programme had to fit in with other calls on capacity and labour at a time when 'resources were stretched to their limit'. The project employed 45,000 labourers nationwide, many of them skilled men such as welders and scaffolders needed in other sectors; it used 90,000 tons of steel, at a time when shipbuilding and repairs were high priorities. The potentially disastrous strains that these demands could have placed on the war economy were mitigated by spreading the production around between contractors in different parts of the country. Contractors in Hampshire, however, played a disproportionately large part in this programme, as exemplified in the PHOENIX programme and in the responsibility for assembling many of the components immediately before the invasion. In this respect, the industrial contribution reflected the contribution of Hampshire's infrastructure.

Conclusion

When approaching the history of Hampshire's logistical contribution to the planning and execution of OVERLORD, it is impossible not to be struck by the scale of the achievements. General Eisenhower's naval aide, Captain Harry Butcher, wrote of the PLUTO scheme that it would 'in itself be regarded as a considerable enterprise in normal times', and these words can be applied to the various other industrial contributions and supply responsibilities taken on by private and public agencies in Hampshire. When the abnormal wartime circumstances are considered, the achievements become all the more considerable. For example, components for the MULBERRY harbours were built in docks alongside regular ship work; passenger trains had to keep on running on the Southern Railway's lines that were moving the invading force southwards; their workshops at Eastleigh had to continue to build trains alongside the orders for glider tail pieces and tank parts. The whole operation stretched an already taut economy, and somehow found some slack in it.

Another remarkable feature of the county's contribution, which was mirrored throughout the country, can be seen in the way in which speedy improvisations were made in order to facilitate various tasks. In the economy of a country in a state of total war, adaptation and improvisation are inevitable, and these can be seen to have happened again and again on the local level in Hampshire up to and after D-Day. The amount of space given over to the invasion force and its equipment, for example, was unprecedented, and called on the conversion of non-military areas into encampments, dumps and vehicle parks: common land, suburban streets and main roads alike were given over to the accommodation of men and machines. Another form of spatial improvisation can be seen in the three beach sites that were used for MULBERRY, where construction sites and suitable slipways had to be built in weeks so that the components could be built and floated. And no summary of improvisation would be complete without reference to the heterogeneous workforce that built the harbours, encompassing imported skilled workers, conscripted local teenagers and middle-aged men, and men from 'the most unlikely quarters [including] pimps and flower-sellers'. Through juggling and improvisation, the industries concerned maintained an effort that was to provide a solid base for Operation OVERLORD. Although the exact contribution of individual elements has been questioned, such as the debate over MULBERRY, the sum of Hampshire's contribution cannot but be seen as paramount to the overall success of the western Allies' invasion of Europe. Without the railways, the ports and the industrial contribution from Hampshire, the strategic choice of Normandy would not have been tenable.

CHAPTER THREE

THE MILITARY PREPARATIONS

Ken Ford

Hampshire's main role in the events surrounding the liberation of Europe was to provide a base from which the assault force could leave for Normandy. It was not the only base, for other forces set sail to France from most of the south coast counties but it was the most important base. Britain provided over half of the forces that landed in Normandy on D-Day and most of them sailed from the Hampshire ports surrounding the Solent.

In 1942 everyone was calling for the 'second front' to take place, but no one knew for sure if there ever was really going to be an invasion of France. If there was, then Southampton and Portsmouth were both bound to be involved in it. Of this there was no doubt. The facilities of the great ports and the surrounding sheltered waterways would be essential if any large-scale combined operations attack was to be made against the enemy. But, before this could happen, the authorities had to have a clear appreciation of just what the coastal ports and their hinterland could handle by way of stores, troops and equipment.

Organising Hampshire for D-Day

Well in advance of any invasion plans, the War Office and Admiralty began their survey of the area. In April 1942, the capacity of Southampton as a base for an amphibious attack was listed as 48 berths for tank landing craft and 75 for assault landing craft. It was a start, but hardly the capacity required to launch the great crusade that would be necessary to gain a foothold on the continent of Europe. Following close behind the naval surveyors came the army. They saw Southampton not only in terms of port facilities and loading points, but as an assembly and concentration area for vast numbers of troops and equipment, prior to embarkation. To encompass this requirement, they looked to the suburbs and beyond.

Suitable sites needed to be found that could be converted into marshalling areas. Sites with open access to good road networks and yet still capable of concealment from enemy air reconnaissance. Just north of the centre of Southampton was the town's major recreation area, the Common: 375 acres of rural countryside surrounded by suburbia. The site was ideal. There was plenty of tree cover, it would be easy to secure the area from the outside world and it was located within a few miles of the docks. The Common was to form one of the most important camps within the area. Other locations, all lying within a 12-mile radius of the town were viewed by the army and those meeting the selection criteria were earmarked as part of the Southampton marshalling area. Given the designation, AREA C, the district stretched in an arc around the landward side of Southampton from Romsey in the west to Hedge End in the east, with its most northerly point centred on Bushfield Camp just south of Winchester.

Clearly, to make best use of the port it had to be worked at full capacity. The marshalling areas

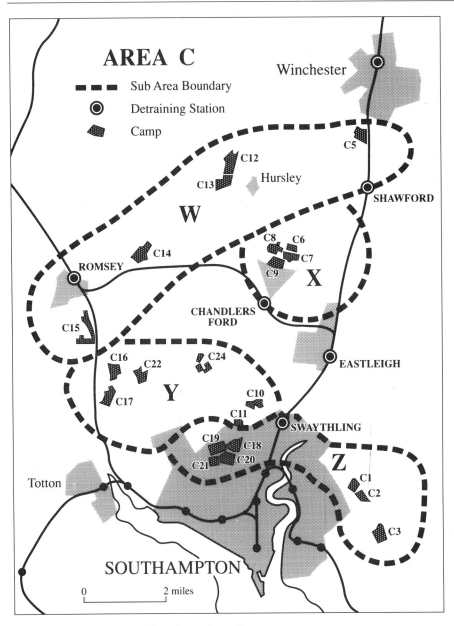

The Southampton Marshalling Area: Area C

would need to be large enough to supply that capacity. On paper, the army estimated that AREA C was capable of accommodating around 12,000 troops. But first there was much work to be done. For AREA C to cope, a vast building programme had to be put in hand. Camps, depots, slipways, security systems, fuel dumps, workshops, roads and rail yards capable of handling thousands of servicemen and millions of tons of stores and equipment all had to be erected. This work was destined to turn Southampton and its district into the largest naval and military base of all time.

In July 1943, an exercise was held to test the capability of AREA C. Troops were transported into the area, held in the reception camps, bussed to the docks and then embarked upon ships. The results were very significant. It was calculated that 11,000 troops could be embarked on each tide. With four high tides a day in the port, the docks could clearly handle up to 44,000 troops a day. AREA C was consequently up-rated to match the port's handling capacity. By D-Day, this number had increased to 53,750 men and 7,070 vehicles. More sites, more camps, more slipways and more roads were required to handle them all.

The same kind of survey was carried out in the Portsmouth area. Although Portsmouth dockyard was

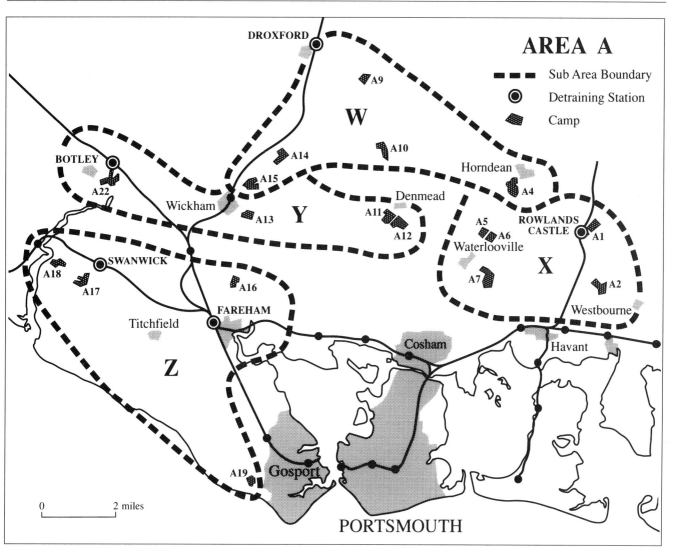

AREA A

- ▬ ▬ ▬ Sub Area Boundary
- ◎ Detraining Station
- Camp

DROXFORD

A9

W

BOTLEY

A22

A14

A15

Wickham

A13

Y

A10

Denmead

A11

A12

Horndean

A4

A5

A6

Waterlooville

A7

ROWLANDS CASTLE

A1

X

A2

Westbourne

SWANWICK

A18

A17

A16

FAREHAM

Titchfield

Z

Cosham

Havant

A19

Gosport

PORTSMOUTH

0   2 miles

The Portsmouth Marshalling Area: Area A

a military port catering for the building, repair and supply of naval vessels, there were many suitable sites within Portsmouth Harbour and the surrounding shoreline that could be adapted for the embarkation of troops and equipment. Spithead and the Solent were ideal protected anchorages for the build-up of invasion vessels. The countryside

A Churchill is loaded onto an LST at the Hardway, Portsmouth (ENHT)

around the city and its environs was carefully studied by the planners and a great marshalling area laid out. Designated AREA A, the army originally estimated that the site should be able to handle 16,000 troops. By D-Day, the actual number being accommodated in AREA A had risen to 29,000.

AREA A was equally as large as AREA C, stretching around Portsmouth from Botley in the west to Westborne in the east, with its northerly point resting on the railway station at Droxford. Major sites for embarkation were designated along the Gosport Peninsula, Portsmouth and Langstone Harbours and Southsea. Once again, a great number of slipways and hards needed to be constructed to cater for the estimated 2,500 vessels that were expected to take part in the operation.

The purpose of slipways and hards, other than for building and repairing ships, was for the loading of landing craft. These assault vessels came in a range of sizes and were designed to perform various functions. The bulk of these specialised landing craft were made up of those which allowed tanks and infantry to be landed directly onto the beach. Built with shallow draughts, the craft were able to run up onto the beach and disgorge their cargoes onto the shore through large doors and ramps in the bows. They then waited for the next high

Pressure on Southampton Docks before D-Day (HJC)

tide to float them off again. They did not need to berth at conventional quays for loading, but could pull onto sloping concrete ramps (hards) to allow tanks to be driven straight on board.

The number of hards and slipways existing in the Southampton Port Area recorded in February 1943 was nine. A building programme to provide many more was started almost immediately and by May 1944 the number had risen to 23. Four of these new hards were within the dockyard complex, whilst the remainder were along the tidal reaches of the River Itchen and Southampton Water, many of which were at local boat-builder's yards such as Thornycroft's at Woolston and Camper and Nicholson's at Northam.

Berthing space at the ports was also at a premium. With the influx of landing craft and supply vessels ranging from large ocean-going ships to small barges, space needed to be found to berth them all. For much of the time, especially with regard to assault landing craft after they had been prepared and kitted out for the attack, they would then need to be anchored to await the time when they would be called forward to be loaded with men and equipment for the invasion. These stationary vessels could not be allowed to obstruct day-to-day port movements, so anchorages had to be found out of the main berthing areas.

Amongst all of this activity, Southampton continued with its normal port activities until just before D-Day. It was not until 13th May 1944 that the docks were shut to incoming cargo traffic. Some of the landing craft were towed around to the Beaulieu river and were moored in its upper reaches. Extra piles were driven into the Itchen at Northam for more craft to be secured. Many new mooring buoys were provided throughout Southampton Water and the River Hamble. The waters around Calshot,

---

CITY OF WINCHESTER

On the battlefields of Normandy our men are sacrificing their

ALL.

You are asked to sacrifice but

LITTLE.

SAVE WATER

"IT ALL DEPENDS ON YOU!"

P. H. WARWICK, Water Engineer.

The demand for water, 24th June 1944 (HC)

Redbridge, Woolston, Northam, Cracknore and Marchwood all had rows of landing craft bobbing at anchor. The same was true for the Portsmouth area. Both Langstone and Portsmouth Harbours and Spithead were almost completely covered with ships and assault craft.

By 1943, the whole of Hampshire had become one vast military area. Building work was being carried out at a furious pace. The infrastructure of the county was being requisitioned, expanded and upgraded in order to cope with the increasing numbers of people arriving in the area to prepare for OVERLORD. The

influx of service personnel and the commandeering of resources by the military had caused a great strain on all of the support services. Things that were normally provided without much thought, such as the supply of water, the treatment of sewage, the electricity network, the telephone and postal system, public transport, places of entertainment and a myriad of other facilities, all needed to re-examine their operations to ensure that the needs of the military took priority. To give just one instance of this, the Southampton Water Undertaking pumped 10,616,000 gallons a day in June 1939; by June 1944 this had risen to 16,670,000 gallons a day. The same rate of expansion was true for all other public undertakings.

The materials with which to build this vast military assembly had to be transported into the area. At that time most commercial traffic was carried by the railways. The rail network of the Southern Railway covered the whole of the south coast. In Hampshire the company also owned Southampton Docks. This great port depended heavily on the rail system to handle incoming and outgoing freight. Few supplies were carried by road, except for local distribution. With Southampton having been selected as the major port for the invasion, the work of the Southern Railway in the area expanded considerably.

Railway installations in Hampshire were already playing a great part in the war effort by supplying their expertise and facilities to other industries. Eastleigh owed its very existence to the railways, with large workshops and marshalling yards dominating the area to the east of the town.

Just north of Eastleigh Railway Station, to the east of the main London to Southampton line, were the marshalling yards. Sixteen sidings were given over to the handling of OVERLORD traffic, with eight others being assigned as reserves for the follow-up stages of the invasion. The traffic normally handled by Eastleigh was transferred to two other new yards at Micheldever and Brockenhurst. Seven new sidings were constructed at Brockenhurst on land that had previously been forest. At Micheldever 17 were built, where before the war there had been none. The Micheldever Marshalling Yards were home to an Ordnance Emergency Depot, staffed by hundreds of soldiers. The shunting crews worked around the clock dealing with requisitions for supplies. Along the side of a huge cutting was a shed over 2,000 ft long. It was said that orders for stores received by late afternoon were packaged and left the depot on the 4.00 a.m. goods train the next day.

At Longparish new sidings were

A Bren gunner prepares in camp at Denmead, Hants (IWM).

built to serve the bomb dumps. Traffic there rose from 478 wagons in December 1943 to 1451 by April 1944. But it was at Lockerley, a few miles north-west of Romsey, that the most remarkable siding was located. Just outside of the tiny station of Dunbridge, with its platform lit by oil lamps and its water supplied by the pub next door, was the great storehouse of the American Army with 15 miles of sidings and 134 covered sheds. The depot was begun in October 1943 and was set in the woods among overhanging trees for partial concealment. The yards made up one of the biggest supply dumps in the country, stockpiling thousands of tons of stores in preparation for the invasion. Before the war, Dunbridge had handled 182 wagons a month.

Protective measures: a smokescreen laid at Southampton Docks, 13th April 1944 (IWM)

for the aircraft. Accommodation was quite primitive, usually tented, with any existing building in the vicinity being requisitioned for use by head-quarters and administration staff. The runways were made up of heavy steel mesh, pinned into the ground to give a stable surface.

Seventy two sites in southern England were originally considered as ALGs in 1942, of which 23 were actually built. All had to be ready for service by 1st April 1944 but many were already completed by the middle of 1943. The airfields were not used operationally until after April 1944. Indeed, in order to preserve the security of the sites, air force units were banned from even visiting them until that date. Four of these ALGs were built in Hampshire at Needs Ore Point, Winkton, Bisterne and Lymington, all of which were in the New Forest. Their role was to provide landing grounds for fighter-bomber aircraft attacking targets in Northern France. In the run-up to D-Day, three of the air-fields, Bisterne, Lymington and Winkton, were used by the USAAF, whilst Needs Ore Point was used by the RAF.

By the middle of 1943, South-ampton had recovered as a port after the bombings of 1941-42 and was back to its pre-war capacity. During that year the amount of cargo discharged by Southampton made it the leading port in Britain

In July 1944, the figure had risen to 5,246. Freight movements at Lockerley built up to a peak around D-Day and then began to tail off rapidly as supplies from the USA were sent direct to France. By October 1944, it had achieved its purpose and traffic at Dunbridge had almost reverted back to pre-war levels.

Another part of the build-up for D-Day that led to a great deal of increased railway traffic was the expansion of activities at aero-dromes along the south coast. In addition to existing permanent air-fields which were enlarged and modernised, many temporary Advanced Landing Grounds (ALG) were built. These airfields were only intended to be used during the sum-mer months in direct support of mil-itary operations in France. They had neither hard runways nor any stand-ing buildings, other than occasional blister hangers. Their specification called for two runways of around 4,000 ft in length at 90 degrees to each other and some hard standings

Canadian troops in camp (IWM)

and the third in the world. Southampton's role in the coming invasion was two-fold: first, it was the principal site for the assembly and launching of the amphibious assault itself; second, it was to act as the major port for the continued supply of troops into the bridgehead and beyond. Whilst the activities at most other ports and assembly areas involved in D-Day would decrease after the invasion, those of Southampton would continue unabated until the end of the war.

In the main, this continued activity was geared towards American needs. Southampton was designated as the major port for the movement and supply of the American forces in north-west Europe. The US 14th

Military movement control: painting parking signs at Wickham, Hampshire (IWM)

Major Port arrived at the dockyards in 1943 and began gearing itself for the coming invasion. By this time the running of the port and its undertakings had became very complex, for there were a number of organisations all trying to put together their own particular piece of the giant puzzle that made up the OVERLORD plan. In addition to the Americans were the Southern Railway (which owned and operated the port), the Royal Navy in the shape of the Flag Officer-in-Charge Southampton (who handled naval movements) and the army's Military Movement Control (which channelled troops into the area and organised their supply and embarkation). To complicate matters, demand for space and facilities within the dockyard was further exacerbated by the commercial undertakings of such private companies as Harland and Wolff and Thornycroft with their shipbuilding and repair work. And then there was the building of the two great engineering projects MULBERRY and PLUTO. All of these activities added to the complexity of the operations surrounding OVERLORD and Southampton. As D-Day approached, the port of Southampton was nearing a state of saturation.

For the invasion ports of Southampton and Portsmouth to work at full efficiency, they needed a constant supply of men and equipment to be fed into the embarkation points at the same rate as ships arrived to transport them away. It was an operation that required a great deal of forward planning and strict control procedures. Both of the ports were in areas that contained activities unrelated to the OVERLORD plan. The local civilian population had to be free to go about their daily life unmolested by the activities going on around them. Whilst the military could close roads and create large one-way circulatory systems for short periods, the needs of the local inhabitants could not be permanently denied. It was impossible to run the whole area as a strict military camp all of the time; some recognition of civilian rights had to be maintained. There needed to be a spirit of co-operation between the needs of the services and the needs of the public. The key to this co-operation was in the organisation of the marshalling areas (AREA A and AREA C) behind the ports.

The composition and location of **AREA A** and **AREA C**, together with their sub-areas **W**, **X**, **Y** and **Z** and their camps, were as follows:

PORTSMOUTH MARSHALLING
AREA A Headquarters – Roche Court, Fareham.

AREA A, Sub-Area W, Headquarters – Bury Lodge, Hambledon.
AREA A, Sub-Area W, Camp A4 – Horndean.
AREA A, Sub-Area W, Camp A9 – Grenville Hall, Droxford.
AREA A, Sub-Area W, Camp A10 – Bury Lodge, Hambledon.
AREA A, Sub-Area W, Camp A14 – Woodend, Soberton Heath.
AREA A, Sub-Area W, Camp A15 – Wickham.
AREA A, Sub-Area X, Headquarters – Queen's Enclosure, Cowplain.
AREA A, Sub-Area X, Camp A1 – Southleigh Forest.
AREA A, Sub-Area X, Camp A2 – Southleigh Forest.
AREA A, Sub-Area X, Camp A5 – Queen's Enclosure, Cowplain.
AREA A, Sub-Area X, Camp A6 – Queen's Enclosure, Cowplain.
AREA A, Sub-Area X, Camp A7 – Waterlooville.
AREA A, Sub-Area Y, Headquarters – Wickham Common.
AREA A, Sub-Area Y, Camp A11 – Bunkers Hill, Denmead.
AREA A, Sub-Area Y, Camp A12 – Bunkers Hill, Denmead.
AREA A, Sub-Area Y, Camp A13 – Wickham Common.
AREA A, Sub-Area Y, Camp A22 – Fairthorne Manor, Botley.
AREA A, Sub-Area Z, Headquarters – Coldeast Hospital, Sarisbury.
AREA A, Sub-Area Z, Camp A16 – Roche Court, Fareham.
AREA A, Sub-Area Z, Camp A17 – Locks Heath.
AREA A, Sub-Area Z, Camp A18 – Sarisbury.
AREA A, Sub-Area Z, Camp A19 – Gosport.

SOUTHAMPTON MARSHALLING
AREA C Headquarters – Glen Eyre, Bassett.

AREA C, Sub-Area W, Headquarters – Hursley Park.
AREA C, Sub-Area W, Camp C5 – Bushfield Camp, Winchester.
AREA C, Sub-Area W, Camp C12 – Hursley Park.
AREA C, Sub-Area W, Camp C13 – Hursley Park.
AREA C, Sub-Area W, Camp C14 – Ampfield.
AREA C, Sub-Area W, Camp C15 – Broadlands Park, Romsey.
AREA C, Sub-Area X, Headquarters – Cranbury Park, Otterbourne.
AREA C, Sub-Area X, Camp C6 – Cranbury Park, Otterbourne.
AREA C, Sub-Area X, Camp C7 – Hiltingbury, Chandlers Ford.
AREA C, Sub-Area X, Camp C8 – Cranbury Park, Otterbourne.
AREA C, Sub-Area X, Camp C9 – Hiltingbury, Chandlers Ford.
AREA C, Sub-Area Y, Headquarters – Chilworth Manor.
AREA C, Sub-Area Y, Camp C10 – Hardmore Copse, Bassett.
AREA C, Sub-Area Y, Camp C11 – Glen Eyre, Bassett.
AREA C, Sub-Area Y, Camp C16 – Nightingale Wood, Rownhams.
AREA C, Sub-Area Y, Camp C17 – Grove Place, Nursling.
AREA C, Sub-Area Y, Camp C22 – Nightingale Wood, Rownhams.
AREA C, Sub-Area X, Camp C24 – Chilworth.
AREA C, Sub-Area Z, Headquarters – The Common, Southampton.
AREA C, Sub-Area Z, Camp C1 – Harefield, Southampton.
AREA C, Sub-Area Z, Camp C2 – Thornhill Park, Southampton.
AREA C, Sub-Area Z, Camp C3 – Netley Common, Southampton.
AREA C, Sub-Area Z, Camp C18 – East Common, Southampton.
AREA C, Sub-Area Z, Camp C19 – West Common, Southampton.
AREA C, Sub-Area Z, Camp C20 – The Common, Southampton.
AREA C, Sub-Area Z, Camp C21 – West Common, Southampton.

There already were permanent barracks established in the concentration areas around the ports, especially at Portsmouth. As the home of the Royal Navy, it had always been something of a garrison town with a good deal of military accommodation. These facilities were already in use by existing units when the planners came to mark out the areas required for the invasion, so AREAS A and C had to be constructed from scratch.

The marshalling areas consisted of a number of individual camps located in sites within a few miles of the ports. There were 18 camps in AREA A, with 22 camps in AREA C. Each of the camps had a similar lay out. The accommodation was arranged in blocks of 50 tents, sub-divided into villages of ten.

Each tent held ten enlisted men, with separate accommodation for NCOs and officers. The camps were almost completely self-contained with their own dining areas, cookhouses, stores, latrines and entertainment areas, all linked together by paths and roadways. Surrounding the encampment, to regulate all personnel entering or leaving the camps, were barbed-wire security fences. Vehicle hard standings were prepared for lorries, armoured cars, tanks and equipment. Trenches were dug as protection against air attack and camouflage netting was strung among the trees to help conceal the site.

The camps were grouped together in sub-areas, each with its own organisational headquarters. There were four sub-areas to each main area, labelled W,X,Y and Z. Every sub-area contained at least one railway station (detraining station) through which the troops arrived into the district. For AREA A, the detraining stations were Botley, Fareham, Droxford, Wickham, Swanwick and Rowlands Castle. For AREA C they were Winchester, Shawford, Eastleigh, Swaythling and Romsey. From these railheads, convoys of lorries shuttled along designated roads carrying the men into the rural camps. Many of the roads feeding the camps were narrow, normally only used to dealing with small volumes of local traffic. Military convoys were slow, wide and cumbersome. To increase safety and to speed up movement, many of these roads were designated one-way only.

Where the roads were wide and safe, they were often allocated for parking and used as hard standings by lorries and tanks. Many miles of Hampshire roads were made full use of in this way. In some cases it was the quiet side streets in towns such as Southampton and Gosport that held lines of vehicles, nose to tail amongst the front gardens and back alleyways of the housing estates. Elsewhere, major roads and dual carriageways harboured squadrons of tanks and detachments of guns. The Winchester by-pass, the A27 at Bursledon, the sea front at Lee-on-the-Solent and the section of the A3 between Horndean and Waterlooville were some of the more notable stretches of road given over to the military.

With so much extra transport using the main roads, special traffic posts were placed at major cross roads to help regulate and control the flow. Convoys of vehicles needed to criss-cross the area to get to the right camps at the right time. The traffic posts helped ensure that whenever one route crossed another, vehicles did not get mixed up. They also helped to keep security within the marshalling area very tight and deterred the unauthorised movement of vehicles. Traffic entering the marshalling areas by road from the rest of the country, had to pass through road convoy regulating points at strategic locations on the periphery of the zone.

In addition to the camps, further sites within the marshalling areas were requisitioned to hold various stores, workshops and dumps. A complete framework of military service corps establishments needed to be constructed to keep the camps supplied and the troops made ready for the attack. Petrol and oil dumps, vehicle workshops, ordnance depots, ammunition supply depots, repair sections, quartermaster stores, field bakeries, field hospitals, embarkation supply depots and so on, all needed their piece of the Hampshire countryside on which to settle. As the camps were built, it was time for the military to move in. First to arrive were the men who were to run the camps. In the case of AREA C, the permanent staff administering the sites was equally composed of British and American units. This was because, although the initial assault troops were entirely British, the majority of the follow-up troops would be American.

The Allied invasion of Normandy was to be the greatest amphibious assault ever undertaken. The planners knew this and they also knew that there was bound to be a high number of casualties both during the attack and in the subsequent campaign to liberate Europe. A sad but necessary requirement for the planning of any battle is to provide essential facilities to receive the wounded. So it was with OVERLORD. Once the fleets had sailed from their Hampshire ports, there would be a momentary lull in activities. The immediate follow-up troops for the invasion were sailing

Handling the wounded: US ambulances disembark in Normandy (IWM)

from other UK ports. From the evening of D-Day itself, the dockyards of Portsmouth and Southampton were to be given over to the reception of wounded men from the beaches of Normandy.

All hospitals in the area, no matter what their normal peace-time role might be, were organised to receive some of the casualties. No one was sure as to what the number

of injured troops might be. One pessimistic forecaster suggested that there could be up to 50% casualties among the men of the airborne assault alone. The most urgent cases were to be sent directly to the main military hospitals, the Royal Naval Hospital at Haslar and the Royal Victoria Hospital at Netley. Both of these hospitals were, however, in an area that would be vulnerable to enemy bombing should he decide to attack the coastal ports in retaliation for the invasion. It was therefore decided that the less urgent cases should be dispatched directly to other hospitals inland, such as those at Winchester and Basingstoke. To supplement the main hospitals, field and transit hospitals were set up throughout AREAs A and C to be prepared for the worst expectations.

The Royal Victoria Hospital at Netley had had a long history of nursing the wounded from many wars. The great Victorian building contained 138 wards and held over 1,000 beds. On 1st April 1944, it was taken over by the Americans and became US Naval Base Hospital No.

12. In the period April 1944 to July 1945, it handled over 4,000 patients whilst in American hands. Immediately after the invasion, during June, July and August, it treated over 500 servicemen, 54% of whom had been wounded in action.

Southwick: Nerve Centre for D-Day

General Eisenhower arrived back in England from the Mediterranean to take up his duties as Supreme Commander on 15th January 1944. He did not want his headquarters (SHAEF) to be situated in the centre of London with all of its diversions and distractions, and so, on the

6th March he moved his team into tented accommodation on the outskirts of the capital at Bushey Park, Teddington. Given the codename WIDEWING, the planning of OVERLORD went on without respite. Montgomery had joined the headquarters of the 21st Army Group at St Paul's School in London on 3rd January 1944. Air Chief Marshal Leigh-Mallory had his headquarters at Stanmore and the Commander of the Allied Naval Expeditionary Force, Admiral Sir Bertram Ramsay, was based in London.

Each of these separate services concentrated on their own role in the operation, under the co-ordination of the Supreme Commander and SHAEF. As the time for the invasion approached, it was necessary to bring their commanders together in an advance command post where the final, important decisions could be made. A search had been going on for some time to find a suitable location along the south coast, preferably in Hampshire near to the Royal Navy's premier port, Portsmouth. Southwick House, a cement-faced Victorian mansion re-styled by Sydney Howell in 1841, was chosen for the task.

The house was set in the extensive wooded grounds of Southwick Park, five miles north of Portsmouth. It had been requisitioned by the Royal Navy in September 1941 to re-house the Navigation School from its

Southwick House: the Advanced Command Post for D-Day (PCS)

The Allied Commanders at Southwick House. Left to right: Lieut. General Omar Bradley, Admiral Sir Bertram Ramsay, Air Chief Marshal Sir Arthur Tedder, General Dwight D. Eisenhower, General Sir Bernard Montgomery, Air Marshal Sir Trafford Leigh-Mallory, Lieut. General W. Bedell-Smith (IWM)

bombed-out site in Portsmouth. Situated just below the great Portsdown Ridge that overlooked the city and the naval dockyard, the site was ideal. A few miles away were the old Palmerston forts of Widley and Southwick. In 1944, the former was an accommodation facility, the latter serving as the communications headquarters of

Admiral Sir Charles Little, Commander-in-Chief Portsmouth Command. Communica-tions facilities were of prime consideration for the siting of the Advance Command Post, and the proximity of both the dockyard and Fort Southwick helped seal the fate of Southwick Park. The grounds of the house were laid out with wide avenues,

Mobility in war: a Map Reproduction Trailer for the US Army lands from the Stephen C Foster at Southampton on 11th November 1943 (ABP Southampton)

lawns and gardens, giving adequate space to allow for the temporary accommodation of the various headquarters' staff. The abundance of tree cover provided excellent camouflage for the top secret site. The house had already been designated as a headquarters building for Admiral Ramsay and it made good sense for all of the SHAEF team to join him there when the time came.

The Navigation School moved out of Southwick Park for Greenwich on 3rd April 1944. On 26th of that month, the Allied Naval Task Force Commander and his staff left their London base and set up their new battle headquarters in the house. What was once a pleasant country estate soon became a large military camp of Nissen huts, caravans and tents, complete with new water and sewage pipes, drains, power supplies, communications systems and welfare and messing facilities for hundreds of service personnel from privates to generals and from able-seamen to admirals.

Admiral Ramsay took up residence in the house itself, with most of his staff located in Nissen huts in the grounds. At the front of the house was the Operations Room where Ramsay would control NEPTUNE, the amphibious side of the invasion. From this room, on a plotting table in the centre and on a large map on the wall, the progress of the invasion fleet would be charted as it moved out across the Channel.

The administrative headquarters of the 21st Army Group began its move to Southwick towards the end of April. At the same time, the Group's tactical headquarters was established. This was composed of the communications facilities, caravans and tented accommodation for the commander and his operational staff. Totally transportable, it allowed Montgomery to be close to the battlefield as the front line progressed through Europe. Separate from the administrative headquarters, this was very much a mobile headquarters. It was established just outside Southwick Park in a modest Georgian building, Broomfield House, located two miles to the east of the village in the shadow of Fort Widley. Monty, and his Chief of Staff, Major General Sir Francis de Guingand, took up residence in the house, whilst his field staff were billeted in tents and caravans in the grounds.

Final preparations

At the end of April, movement orders went out to the assault units who were to land in France on D-Day. In response they began moving towards the south coast and into the marshalling areas. At the same time, the naval force that was to carry the troops into the attack, together with their protective screen of minesweepers and destroyers, began to assemble in the various ports of embarkation. Space was at a premium as the dockyards, creeks, estuaries and harbours began to fill with the vast armada. Many vessels had to be berthed up to eight abreast so great was the demand for mooring sites.

The arrival of the assault troops in the marshalling areas of the embarkation ports along the south coast coincided with the application of a coastal ban affecting a belt ten miles deep extending from the Wash to Land's End. In this zone, all persons who were not resident in the Protected Area were banned from entering or being in the area after 1st April 1944. Certain classes of person, such as Members of Parliament, service personnel on duty and government servants at work were given general permission to be in the zone. All other people were banned. Unauthorised movement out of the area was also forbidden. The whole district was cut off from the rest of England. Checks were made at railway stations and on buses and other public vehicles. Places of amusement, hotels and apartment houses were inspected. Any person not carrying his or her identity card was liable to arrest on the spot. As a result of the ban, Portsmouth and Southsea had their quietest Easter

Tanks at Cowplain, Hampshire (IWM)

Troops train for the assault in the Solent area (IWM)

Troops and landing craft practise under the protection of a balloon barrage in the Solent (IWM)

holiday on record. The ban was to remain in force until 25th August.

Not only was the general neighbourhood around the marshalling areas sealed, but so were the camps themselves from time to time. At the end of April and the beginning of May, a series of exercises codenamed FABIUS took place. They were intended to be carried out under conditions as close to the real invasion as possible to test all aspects of the naval plan, NEPTUNE. Once the troops inside the camps had been briefed about the exercises, the camps were sealed just as they would be when the assault troops received their invasion orders prior to D-Day.

Operation FABIUS had six separate stages: FABIUS 1 and V were concerned with the forces based at Portland and around the Thames Estuary, whilst FABIUS II, III and IV tested the assault forces based in AREA A and AREA C. FABIUS VI was concerned with the post-OVER-LORD follow-up process.

FABIUS II, involved the assault force which was to land on GOLD Beach (Force G), the 50th Northumbrian Division. The division was embarked from Southampton and Portsmouth and landed at Hayling Island. FABIUS III exercised Force J, destined for JUNO Beach, when it embarked the 3rd Canadian Division by lifting it from Southampton and

Portsmouth and landing it in Bracklesham Bay. In FABIUS IV, Force S, the British 3rd Division which was set to land at SWORD Beach during the invasion, was embarked from Southampton and Portsmouth and put down at Littlehampton.

FABIUS VI was intended to evaluate the effectiveness of the administration of AREA C and the follow-up phase of the invasion. After the units involved in FABIUS II and III had vacated their camps, American troops moved in to take them over. A few days later, these US troops were moved to the dockyard as though they were embarking to reinforce the bridgehead. They did not actually board ships but were dispersed by road back to their holding camps elsewhere. The process tested the post-invasion role of the marshalling area, monitoring the ability of AREA C to receive and dispatch large num-bers of troops in transit to the front.

Briefing for the FABIUS exercises took two days, with all participants expected to behave exactly as they would during the real thing. In some cases, the troops did not know that they were involved in an exercise and assumed that the count down for the invasion had begun. After briefing came the marshalling process, whereby troops were split up into units and merged with others to form a ship load. This involved moving soldiers and equipment to other camps and organising transport to bring them to the pier heads at the right moment for boarding. This marshalling process took two days. The next four days were taken up by embarkation procedures. The troops and their equipment, guns and tanks were loaded onto landing craft, which then moved away from the berths and hards and were assembled into convoys. This process had to be completed 24 hours before the time of the proposed landings, D-Day minus 1. Then came the sea voyage, just like the real thing. The armada of ships moved out of the Southampton and Portsmouth areas, through the Solent, past Spithead and out into the Channel. At dawn the next day they landed on the exercise beaches. Above them, throughout the whole period, the tactical air forces provided continuous air cover, practising their own methods of protecting marshalling areas and ship convoys.

The FABIUS exercises tested the co-ordination and ability of the land, sea and air forces to implement NEPTUNE and OVERLORD according to plan. It was an opportunity for last minute adjustments to be made and for the lessons learned to be applied. Once these FABIUS simulations were complete, there was nothing more for the troops to do but to wait for the final order to go.

The fleet in review before H.M. King George VI, 24th May 1944 (HMSO)

Choosing the date

Attention now focused on the actual date of the invasion. The troops landing on the beaches on D-Day would be confronted by many underwater obstacles designed to rip the landing craft apart. The NEPTUNE plan allowed for demolition teams to land prior to the main assaults to deal with these obstacles. To do this dryshod, they would have to arrive just ahead of the advancing tide and the incoming troops. The work would also have to be done in daylight. For the air landings, it was desirable for the aircraft to make their approach to the French coast in complete darkness before the moon rose, but the actual drops needed to be made in moonlight in order to locate the landing zones. In effect, D-Day would need to be on a day when half-tide on the east coast of the Bay of the Seine would be just after first light and when the previous night had seen the moon rise between one and two in the morning. Only six to eight days in June 1944 provided these special sets of circumstances.

On 8th May, Eisenhower selected Monday 5th June as the date of the invasion. It was the first day in June when the tides, the moon and the hours of daylight would be at the optimum required for the assault. Final confirmation, however, would depend on the weather. If any postponement was made, then only the next two days, 6th and 7th June, would be suitable for the attack. After that, the moon and tides would conspire against the landings and further delays would be inevitable.

Accurate weather forecasting was

essential for the correct timing of the invasion. The whole operation would be impossible if the minimum acceptable conditions were exceeded. For the attack to take place, the wind should be no greater than Force 3 on shore and Force 4 off shore; cloud base no lower that 3,000 ft with a cover no thicker than 5/10ths and visibility not less than three miles. In the run up to D-Day, Eisenhower held twice weekly conferences with his meteorologists to test their ability to provide accurate forecasts. Led by Group Captain J.M. Stagg, the team was made up of experts from all three of the services from both Britain and the USA.

On 23rd May, Eisenhower confirmed that D-Day was to be 5th June. From the tented camp of SHAEF in Bushey Park the long awaited signal for the start of operation NEPTUNE was transmitted. In response, all along the coast of southern England, the loading of the naval craft which were to take part in the assault began.

Hampshire and the Air Assault

Whilst the Allied armies and navies waited for the signal to launch the invasion, the British and American air forces continued with their attacks on German territory. The two tactical air forces raised in support of the cross-Channel attack, the British Second Tactical Air Force commanded by Air Marshal Sir Arthur Coningham and the US Ninth Air Force commanded by Lieutenant General Lewis Brereton, flew non-stop missions against communications centres, radar stations, gun emplacements and beach defences. In order not to give the enemy any indication that the site of the invasion was Normandy, these attacks were not simply confined to northern France but ranged over the whole of the Channel and North Sea coastlines.

Prior to D-Day, the two tactical air forces moved many of their units to airfields close by the south coast in order to employ their relatively short-range fighter-bombers over the Normandy countryside. The aerodromes of Hampshire, especially those in the New Forest, were ideal for them and most of the air stations in the area hosted at least one formation from these tactical wings. Many of the American squadrons were newly raised, shipped in direct from the USA straight on to operational airfields and into action. Some of them were allocated to green-field sites which were no more than temporary landing strips with primitive accommodation. Four of these temporary airfields in Hampshire, the Advance Landing Grounds of Needs Ore Point, Bisterne, Winkton and Lymington had brief but spectacular

lives. They all became operational around April 1944 but by the middle of July, when airfields in France became available, they had all ceased flying.

Bisterne was home to the men of the American 371st Fighter Group who moved into the airfield direct from the US in March 1944. Their arrival in Europe must have been something of a culture shock for the American airmen, for there were few home comforts available in the tented accommodation around the airfield. The group flew Thunderbolt aircraft on fighter-bomber missions against ground targets in France. On D-Day, aircraft from Bisterne carried out dive-bombing missions in support of troops on the beaches. On 23rd June, the fighters moved across to bases in France and Bisterne ceased work as an operational airfield soon after.

More Thunderbolts operated from Winkton airfield, just to the northwest of Christchurch. The ALG became operational with the arrival of the USAAF 404th Fighter Group on 4th April 1944. Winkton's fighter-bombers attacked ground targets in northern France, including sorties against V-1 rocket sites. On 6th June, they provided high level protection to the landings, flying 191 sorties during the day.

The RAF flew rocket-firing Typhoon aircraft from Needs Ore Point, concentrating on enemy radar and communications installations. On

A De Haviland Mosquito FB XVIII in Invasion Markings (the black and white identification stripes painted on Allied aircraft). Aircraft of this type operated from Lasham against communications targets in the spring of 1944 (IWM)

D-Day itself, 146 Wing flew standing patrols over the lodgement area. The planes were on call to the assault troops on the beaches, available to attack any targets designated by observers on the ground.

Lymington ALG was typical of that type of airfield, having just basic tented accommodation, wire mesh runways and two blister hangars. The USAAF 50th Fighter Group operated from the airfield from March 1944, flying their first operational attack with P-47 Thunderbolts against enemy-held territory on 1st May. The group left for bases in France on 25th June.

In addition to the intense activities taking place on these temporary Advance Landing Grounds, many other Hampshire airfields participated in the pre-invasion attacks on German territory. Altogether there were 30 operational airfields in

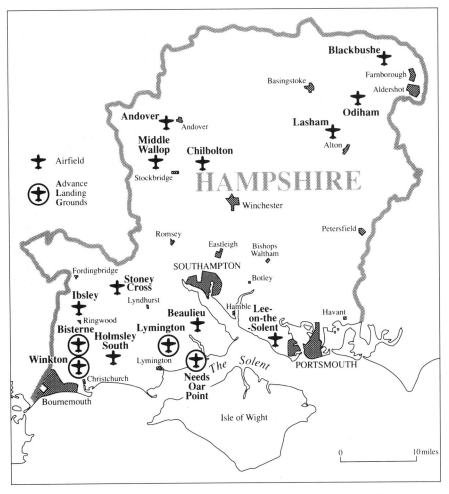

Hampshire airfields operating in support of the landings on 6th June 1944

Hampshire during the Second World War. Many of them were assigned to specific roles not connected with direct offensive action, such as the experimental station at Farnborough, the ferry field at Marwell Hall and the Airspeed factory airfield at Portsmouth. Others had a long history of flying, dating back to the early days of aviation, like the Battle of Britain fighter station at Middle Wallop, the First World War American naval air station at Eastleigh and the pre-war bomber station at Andover. Many more had been built during the early years of the Second World War to cope with the vast expansion of the RAF and the arrival of the USAAF.

On the wild heath-land of the New Forest, three standard three-runway airfields were built during 1941-42, at Holmsley, Stoney Cross and Beaulieu. These large aerodromes were put to a variety of uses during the war by both the RAF and the USAAF, including bombing, transport and fighter operations. All of them played host either to American or Canadian units prior to D-Day and were involved in attacks against targets in northern France. From Holmsley on 6th June, Canadian squadrons from 144 Wing flew in direct support of troops on the beaches. Later that month, a Mosquito from Holmsley made contact with the first V-1 rocket sighted in flight over England. At Beaulieu, the USAAF 365th Fighter Group flew Thunderbolt aircraft in support of ground troops on OMAHA Beach on D-Day, whilst the USAAF 367th Fighter Group provided fighter cover for the invasion force with P-38 Lightnings flying out of Stoney Cross.

Other Hampshire airfields were equally busy playing their part in the pre-invasion build-up. From Middle Wallop, early in 1944, the American 12th, 15th, 107th and 109th Squadrons began carrying out vertical and oblique photography of the whole of the coastline of northern France. Tactical and photo-reconnaissance operations were also carried out by a number of RAF units operating out of Odiham. Lasham airfield hosted Mosquito aircraft from RAF 107 Squadron prior to D-Day, their task being to attack communications targets by night. From 2200 hours on 5th June, aircraft from Lasham bombed road and rail targets all over Normandy. The next evening they did it all again, attacking anything that moved in the interdiction zone around the lodgement area. Andover was given over to the USAAF 307th Fighter Group flying Lightning fighter aircraft. Prior to the invasion the group dive-bombed radar installations. On 6th June they provided cover to the amphibious convoys of the assault troops. The Americans also took over Thruxton airfield in February 1944, when the 366th Fighter Group moved in with their Thunderbolts. On 6th June the group dropped 1,000lb bombs on German heavy gun emplacements in the lodgement area.

More American P-47 Thunderbolts operated out of Christchurch airfield against targets in Normandy when the 405th Fighter Group took over the station in April 1944. At this aerodrome there were a number of accidents caused by heavily laden Thunderbolts attempting to take off from the relatively short runway.

A groundcrewman paints Invasion Markings on a US Marauder medium bomber in preparation for D-Day (IWM)

The worst incident was on 29th June when three aircraft crashed into bungalows on take-off, killing 14 people and injuring 23.

The American 368th Fighter Group moved into Chilbolton airfield on 15th March 1944 and used its P-47s to bomb and strafe German airfields in France. On 6th June it provided close support to ground troops in the bridgehead when it attacked and destroyed five German gun positions with 1,000 lb bombs. The 368th Fighter Group was one of the first units to operate out of airfields in France when it crossed the Channel on 19th June. Chilbolton then provided facilities to transport aircraft, ferrying in wounded American soldiers to a large field hospital outside Stockbridge.

Blackbushe (Hartfordbridge) aerodrome was a bomber station in 1944. Boston medium bombers attacked gun emplacements and V-1 targets prior to D-Day, but on 5th June the bombs were exchanged for smoke-laying dischargers and the aircraft operated around the lodgement area laying smoke to

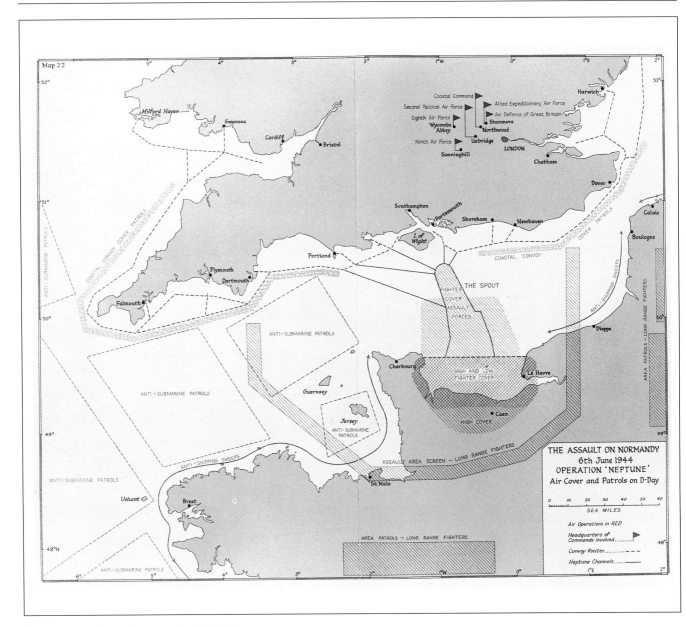

Air cover and patrols on D-Day (HMSO)

A US P38J Lightning fighter of the type flown from Stoney Cross to provide fighter cover for the D-Day landings (IWM)

assist the landing forces. Later that month, aircraft from Blackbushe carried out large-scale raids on German troop positions.

Lee-on-the-Solent airfield was crowded with Seafires, Spitfires and Mustangs from RAF and Fleet Air Arm units prior to D-Day. On the day of the invasion itself, the first aircraft, a pair of Seafires, took off at dawn (0440 hours) to spot targets for the naval guns of the great armada. During that day, the airfield dispatched 435 sorties in support

A B26F Marauder of the Ninth US Air Force attacks German troops in Normandy, June 1944 (IWM)

of the invasion. Lee-on-the-Solent was the busiest D-Day airfield amongst the tactical air force stations. Gosport was the home of the Air Torpedo Development Unit and had a relatively quiet time during the invasion.

As contemporary German comments make clear, the overwhelming nature of the Allied air superiority played a vital part in the success of Operation OVERLORD, in preparing the way for the ground forces to gain a foothold in Normandy.

The last two weeks

D-Day had been set by General Eisenhower for Monday 5th June. On 23rd May, orders were issued for the sealing of the camps. That night, those soldiers administering the marshalling area were joined by other security troops from the 21st Army Group and by morning the camps were closed to all contact with the outside world. Over the next few days, until the troops left for their embarkation points, armed guards patrolled the outer and inner perimeters of the camps. Briefings began on 24th May and lasted for the next five days. It was a very crucial time for all those involved, for each man had to know exactly what was expected of him. Only a very few selected men knew the actual location of the proposed landings, all briefings were carried out using codenames for the objectives. For instance, the landing point of the 1st Battalion of the Hampshire Regiment at Le Hamel near Arromanches, was simply known as GOLD – JIG – GREEN (GOLD Beach, JIG Sector, right hand assault).

On 29th May, the marshalling process began. The various units were gathered together into the groups that would eventually be transported to the ships to form boat loads. Two days were allowed for these manoeuvres; then, on 31st May came the order to load.

A convoy rides at anchor on an evening before D-Day, escorted by a Frobisher class cruiser (private collection)

Final preparations: last minute tests of DUKWs before loading onto LSTs, 5th June 1944 (IWM)

Churchill and Eisenhower review Allied troops at Barton Stacey, Hants (IWM)

The slow, complicated journey to the docks now began, with each convoy allocated to be at the right embarkation point at the correct time, to board the ship that would deposit its allocated payload on the right beach at the precise hour. These groups of vehicles lined all the approaches to the sea. Stretching inland for miles, rows and rows of lorries, guns, tanks and jeeps jammed all roads in the area. Weapons of war sat incongruously among the allotments and back gardens of the local civilian population. Children played games amongst the tanks; women took cups of tea to the waiting troops.

But the locals had seen it all before during countless exercises and had little idea that this was, at last, 'the real thing'.

The loading process had to be completed by the morning of 4th June, so that the great armada could put to sea and set down its powerful cargo on the beaches of Normandy at dawn the next day. All around the Solent, landing craft slipped from their moorings and moved towards the specially built hards to be loaded with their shipment of assault troops and weapons. They slid onto the concrete ramps four at a time with bow doors opened ready to receive the lines of waiting

vehicles. After loading, they resumed their places at the same moorings they had been anchored at for so long. To the enemy, from the air, everything looked as it had done over the previous weeks.

The concentrated activity at the ports and dockyards was matched by equally concerted efforts at the smaller embarkation points. Along the Hamble river at Warsash, most of the commandos involved in the assault climbed aboard their small infantry landing craft. At Gosport, on the newly built hards and slipways Canadian tanks and guns were loaded onto tank landing craft. From the holiday beaches of Southsea, along temporary jetties constructed from scaffolding tubing, long lines of infantry shuffled aboard small boats and were ferried out to large infantry landing ships lying at anchor off Spithead. South Parade Pier was pressed into use to embark more troops. On the other side of Southampton, the tiny port of Lymington hosted still more landing craft.

Eisenhower joined the team at the Advanced Command Post in Southwick a week before the invasion and set up his headquarters in the tree-covered estate. The site was some distance from the mansion on the south side of the park. The Supreme Commander was housed in a spacious caravan containing a living room, kitchen, study and bedroom.

Around the trailer was a tented encampment housing his personal staff and communications team. Inside the caravan, Eisenhower had three telephones: a red one linking him directly to Washington; a black phone connecting him to Southwick House and a green one giving him contact with 10 Downing Street.

The countdown to the invasion now began. Hampshire had become the location of the power base for the liberation of the free world. All of the main commanders now gathered around Eisenhower at Southwick to make the most important decision of them all, the final order to go. The OVERLORD plan had been set in motion by Eisenhower's decision of 23rd May. Preparations to launch the vast sea and air armadas were complete. Ships were loaded with heavy equipment, tanks and armoured cars were waterproofed, aircraft were armed and primed, orders were issued and formations briefed. Everything was ready to touch down on the soil of Normandy on 5th June. The operation now rested on the weather being suitable to carry out the assault.

Friday 2nd June was bright, warm and sunny. The Prime Minister's train pulled into the tiny railway station at Droxford a few miles to the west of Southwick. Churchill had brought members of the war cabinet and overseas leaders with him to meet with the OVERLORD

Commandos load up with the 1st LCI Squadron at Warsash on the Hamble (IWM)

commanders, visit the area and have one last conference with Eisenhower. Droxford was chosen for the meeting because of the proximity of a railway tunnel just outside of the station. In the event of an air raid, the train could back into the tunnel for protection.

With Churchill were the premiers from various countries of the Dominions, including Canada, New Zealand, Rhodesia and South Africa. They all took the opportunity of visiting troop concentrations in the area and to see for themselves the vast fleets of ships at anchor in the Solent.

'Okay, let's go!'

With the amphibious landings set to take place between 0600 and 0700 hours on Monday 5th June, the final decision for the attack to go ahead had to be made at least 24 hours prior to this, that is early Sunday morning. SHAEF's weather forecasters, led by Group Captain Stagg, now became the focus of attention at the Advance Command Post. Regular briefings were required by the Supreme Commander in order to give him as much prior knowledge of the likely weather situation as

The troops depart (IWM)

possible. Working from a Nissen hut at the rear of Southwick House, Stagg and his team charted the courses of weather systems that might affect the landing. The first of these final daily briefings took place on Friday evening at 2130 hours.

The meeting was held in what was the old library of Southwick House but which had been converted into a dining room for the senior mess of Admiral Ramsay's staff. Bare bookcases lined the wall. Dining tables had been pushed out of the way to make room for a number of easy chairs. Eisenhower and his team were sitting comfortably when the chief weatherman entered the room. Stagg's message to them was pessimistic: the likely weather scene for the next few days was potentially full of menace. Fronts out in the Atlantic were bringing a period of very unsettled weather towards the Channel. Such a forecast was too unreliable to warrant calling off the attack and so the Supreme Commander instructed his staff to carry on with the plan as it was.

On Saturday 3rd June the infantry involved in the assault waves of the invasion began to board their ships. Some embarked at Lymington, Southampton, Gosport, Portsmouth and Hamble directly onto smaller vessels, whilst others were ferried out to large ships anchored in the Solent and at Spithead. The same embarkation process was taking place along the coast at Newhaven, Shoreham, Poole, Weymouth, Portland, Torquay and Dartmouth. The first echelons of the great armada began slowly putting out to sea and heading for the assembly area south of the Isle of Wight.

Although the weather outside on Saturday 3rd June started clear and sunny, it began to deteriorate as the day progressed. At 2130 hours that evening, Eisenhower held another conference of his commanders. He asked if Stagg might be more optimistic about the forecast the next day. The answer was negative. Eisenhower decided to make a provisional decision to hold up the operation and to make the final decision early the next morning.

A few hours later the briefing resumed. Those present in the library were the same people as the previous evening. Stagg immediately confirmed that there had been no substantial change to the situation presented earlier and his forecast remained the same. The first depression would hit the area later that day and winds would reach Force 6 in the Channel. There would be 10/10ths cloud for most of the time with heavy showers. The Supreme Commander asked his commanders to weigh up the situation and advise what ought to be done.

From the navy, Admiral Ramsay said he was prepared to go ahead but with some misgivings. Montgomery did not favour any delay. Leigh-Mallory wanted to postpone because of the inability of his bombers to bomb in bad weather. The Deputy Supreme Commander, Tedder, agreed with the Air C-in-C. Two were for the attack to go ahead, two were against. That left Eisenhower to decide the outcome. After careful deliberation he confirmed the earlier postponement and ordered the recall of all those ships at sea. OVERLORD had been put on hold.

As predicted, throughout Sunday the weather worsened. By the evening, high winds had arrived and were buffeting the tents and caravans hidden beneath the trees of the park. The whole of the Advance Command Post was swept with driving rain. At 2100 hours, Eisenhower and his team gathered again to listen to Stagg. Almost unbelievably, Stagg and his team predicted that the weather would improve enough in the next 24 hours to give a short period when the conditions would be very nearly those required to allow the operation to go ahead. Beyond that, it was likely a further depression would arrive from the Atlantic and bring more unsettled weather. The

Preparing for Liberation: Sherman tanks loaded for the assault (IWM)

forecast was just what the assembled team wanted to hear.

Once again Eisenhower went around the room seeking the views of his commanders. This time, their replies were all positive. The Supreme Commander agreed, OVERLORD was back in business and the sea attack would go in at dawn on Tuesday 6th June. The order would be confirmed at anoth-

er meeting in the early hours of the next morning (Monday 5th June) at 0415 hours.

The final decision to set in motion the great invasion to liberate the peoples of northern Europe from German occupation was taken at around 0430 hours that Monday morning. Once again, in the library of Southwick House, the most powerful commanders in the Allied

A convoy leaves Spithead for France, 5th June 1944 (HMSO)

world met to consider the situation. Stagg confirmed that his forecast had not changed and the clear 'slot' in the weather would hold long enough for the sea and airborne assault to take place. Winds along the coast of Normandy would be around Force 3, cloud cover would be 3/10ths or less at a height of 2-3,000 ft and visibility would be good. His audience was delighted and their relief clear for all to see. The air, land and sea commanders all agreed that the attack should go in. Eisenhower deliberated for a moment and then said, 'Okay, let's go.' Operation OVERLORD had been launched.

In Ramsay's War Room, down the hall from the library, the progress of the ships as they set out across the Channel was plotted on the large table in the centre of the room. Even as Eisenhower was making his final decision, the traces were showing the amphibious armada slowly snaking out into the Channel from the myriad of embarkation ports. A few miles away along the crest of Portsdown Hill, the red bricked front of Fort Southwick overlooked the great naval port and the masses of ships lying at anchor in the Solent. Deep beneath its Victorian parade ground, along the steel-lined corridor that led to the operations room, banks of teleprinters remained silently ready for the first messages to arrive from the mainland of Europe. Eisenhower's great crusade had begun. All the world now looked towards the command post set in the rural Hampshire countryside to see if it was to succeed.

On Monday, through seas whipped up by the squally conditions, the lines of ships from the creeks, harbours, ports and dockyards of Hampshire were assembled in larger groups and then into convoys. Finally, they were slotted into position as part of the assault forces of the great armada and set out into the English Channel, Force G through the Needles Passage and Force J past the Nab, on towards Normandy.

At 0725 hours on Tuesday 6th June 1944, the first British seaborne infantry landed on GOLD beach in Normandy. The battalion on the extreme right-hand flank of the assault, the traditional post of honour in an attack, 'the right of the line', hit the waterfront opposite the small village of Le Hamel. Plunging into a tremendous barrage of enemy fire the men fought their way off the beach and spread out to take on the strong-points and defences of Hitler's Fortress Europe. Those men in that attack gained all of their objectives that day at the cost of 182 casualties. It was fitting then that these soldiers who made up the vanguard of the assault should have sailed from the port of Southampton and were the men of the 1st Battalion of the Hampshire Regiment.

CHAPTER FOUR

OPERATION NEPTUNE, THE NAVAL ASSAULT

Alastair Wilson

Hampshire has seen British armies depart for the Continent, usually France, in almost every century since the Norman invasion. It is no coincidence that the ports of Hampshire have been used as the point of departure, because the unique double tides in Southampton Water have given the ports there an advantage when it comes to loading ships with military hardware. So, in a sense, the despatch of the D-Day armies was just another in the long series of expeditionary forces which have been gathered and sent on their way; from Edward III's army in 1346, before the battle of Crécy, to the BEF in 1914, on its way to the trenches of Flanders, all have passed through Hampshire, to take passage under the escort of the King's ships or the Royal Navy.

But the armada which gathered in 1944 was the largest ever seen. 6,833 ships and craft took part, of which 78% were British or Canadian; 17% were American; while the remaining 5% were French, Norwegian, Dutch, Polish and Greek. Not all of them sailed from Hampshire waters, as we shall see, but the whole focus of the invasion lay between Portsmouth and the beaches of Normandy, and all were under the command and control of the Allied Naval Commander-in-Chief, Admiral Sir Bertram Ramsay, KCB, KBE, MVO, who had his headquarters in Southwick Park, H.M.S. *Dryad*.

The invasion involved no major sea battle. The seas and skies of the Channel were effectively controlled by the Royal Navy and the Royal Air Force. Which is not to say that there was no threat from the German Navy. But the German surface fleet had been badly mauled in the Norwegian campaign in 1940 and in subsequent actions. What remained were the U-boats, still a potent force, although they had lost the Battle of the Atlantic the year before, and small craft: destroyers, torpedo boats, mine-sweepers, F lighters (F for Flak – anti-aircraft ships), R boats and E boats (the German equivalent of our motor launches and motor torpedo boats):

all these craft were formidable adversaries; on the whole, the German destroyers carried a heavier armament than our fleet destroyers, while their torpedo boats were very much the equivalent of our small destroyers (the 'Hunt' class).

Until 1944, the U-Boats did not operate in the Channel very much. British minefields denied them passage through the Dover Straits and, in any case, their main targets were the convoys converging on Britain from around the world, out in the Atlantic and up from the Mediterranean. But between 1940 and late 1943, British destroyers and coastal forces fought an unending battle with the German light forces. Our aims were to keep open the coastal convoy routes which were a vital link in Britain's transport system. For example, the south's coal-fired power stations were all supplied by sea. Portsmouth's First Destroyer Flotilla were prominent in many actions, not just 'defensive' (as convoy operations are sometimes inaccurately described) but also in offensive sweeps, along with motor

Admiral Ramsay with his P.A.,
Lt. Henderson, at St Germain,
December 1944 (IWM)

torpedo boats (MTBs) and motor gun boats (MGBs) based in Gosport and elsewhere along the south coast.

By the end of 1943, our light craft had achieved a mastery such that, when the invasion did take place, the German Navy's intervention was of little effect. Nonetheless, 18 major war vessels were lost due to enemy action in the three months ending 6th September 1944, eight by mines, four by U-boats, three by one-man submarines (with a further two damaged, one of which was subsequently scuttled to form part of the MULBERRY breakwater), two by torpedoes from surface ships, and one by aircraft attack. A further two minesweepers were lost as a result of a tragic misidentification by our own aircraft. In the same period, the Germans lost 13 U-boats within the confined waters of the Channel (plus many others in the Bay of Biscay and South-Western Approaches and elsewhere). None of these figures include the losses of minor war vessels on either side.

The Problem

The task of the Navies was to ensure that the Armies were able to comply with the principle of war which was best expressed by the US General Sherman in the Civil War, to the effect that the winner would be the General who 'gits thar fustest with the mostest'. Admiral Ramsay put it in more refined military detail in his message to the invasion fleet on 5th June: 'Our task in conjunction with the Merchant Navies of the United Nations and supported by the Allied Air Forces is to carry the Allied Expeditionary Force to the Continent, to establish it there in a secure bridgehead and to build it up and maintain it at a rate which will outmatch that of the enemy.'

Once the location and size of the assault army had been decided, the planning boiled down to making provision for those three main tasks set out by Admiral Ramsay.

Carrying the army to France involved finding enough ships of the right type to carry the assault forces, organising their loading, sailing, routeing, escorting, through waters which had been swept clear of mines, and final delivery to the right place at the right time. Establishing it there in a secure bridgehead meant holding the ring to prevent enemy forces, whether land or sea, from hindering the build-up of our forces once ashore: so far as the sea was concerned, this meant patrolling round the perimeter of the landing anchorages, and further afield (many of the 13 German submarines destroyed were sunk off the south coast of England); while keeping the German land forces at bay meant provision of overwhelming naval bombardment support for as long as the army was within range – which could be over 15 miles from the beach. And finally, building it up at a rate which outmatched the enemy meant provision of shipping, ports and a tight timetable organisation which delivered the right men and the right stores in the right place at the right time. All these things were achieved in the naval plan, which was given the codename Operation NEPTUNE.

By the time serious planning for OVERLORD began, the Allies had designed and built, and were continuing to build, landing craft of all types: strange looking craft to a seaman but nonetheless effective. Much of this had been the responsibility of Admiral Lord Louis Mountbatten, as Chief of Combined Operations. Lessons had been learnt at the tragedy of Dieppe, and had been applied during the landings in North Africa and Sicily. But the late decision in January 1944 to increase the size of the assault force from three divisions to five meant that there would not be enough craft available at the end of April, and so the assault had to be postponed to allow for one month's extra production of landing craft.

The Plan

Before detailed plans could be made, it was necessary to gather as much intelligence and background information as possible. At one level, this involved examining family holiday snaps from happy days in France before the war, which helped to judge the nature of the beach, its gradient and a host of other minor factors, which all went to make up the overall picture: air reconnaissance played its part, as did the information from the Free French Navy, whose main barracks were at Emsworth. But the most

"...now 'ere we 'ad a saying, 'all ship-shape'; but it seems to 'ave lost its meaning lately.' – Navy News' view of combined operations craft (Punch)

hard won information came from the hydrographic surveyors, swimmers and canoeists of various specialist units, such as Forfar force, which operated out of Warsash, and particularly the Combined Operations Pilotage Parties, from Hayling, who regularly carried out precision surveying close to the enemy coast, sometimes landing, to bring back samples of the materials which made up the various beaches. Just as importantly, they discovered the

nature of the obstacles which the Germans were laying all along the coast.

Out of all this, the overall naval plan took shape. The size of the assault force meant that it was not possible for it to be loaded in one port. Each of the five assault divisions was allocated one beach, and its own landing force. The landing forces took their name from the initial of the beach's codename: so, from east to west, there were SWORD

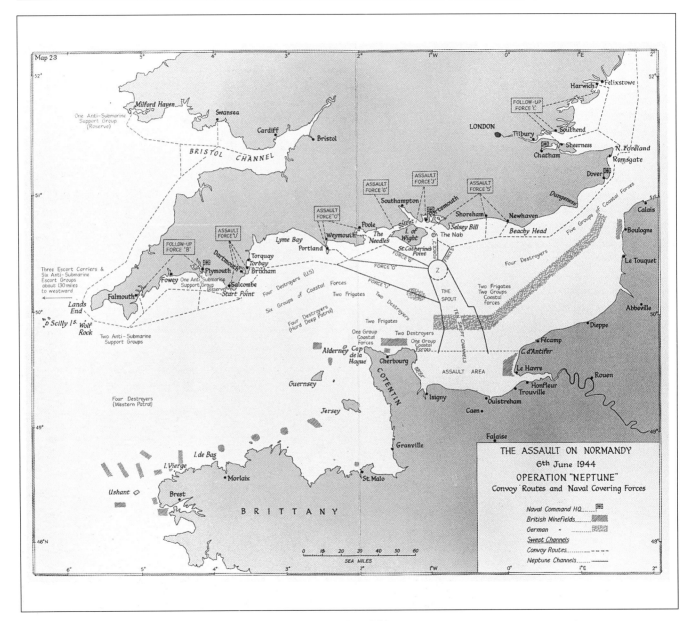

Assault forces, convoy routes and naval cover, 6th June 1944 (HMSO)

beach, Force S, which sailed from Portsmouth and Sussex ports; JUNO beach, Force J, whose shore HQ were in the Royal Yacht Squadron in Cowes; GOLD beach, Force G, which sailed out of the western Solent from its loading points in Southampton Water, the Beaulieu river, and Lymington. For OMAHA beach, Force O came from Weymouth, and for UTAH beach, Force U came the longest distance, from Plymouth.

In turn, each landing force was subdivided. As an example, Force G had three sections, carrying respectively the assault troops, the support troops, and the reserve troops. Each landing force had its own bombardment support force and minesweeping force. The three landing forces in the British sector were combined to form the eastern Task Force, under Rear-Admiral Sir Philip Vian. Other forces under the Task Force Commander's command were the smaller destroyers, MTBs and MLs which provided the anti-submarine escorts and anti-E-boat patrols.

The plan called for most of the landing forces to pass through a concentration area, Area Z, some 10 miles in diameter, 20 miles south-east of the Isle of Wight. From here, 10 swept channels led southwards to the assault area. For the passage over, each force had a 'slow' lane and a 'fast' lane, and ships were timed to sail so that both the slow

Loading for the assault: DUKWs embark at the Hardway, Portsmouth (IWM)

Loading US trucks into an LST, possibly at Weymouth (private collection)

LST and LCT at the Hardway, Portsmouth (ENHT)

and fast ships arrived at the same time.

The ships of the bombardment force were to be allocated specific targets. In the first assault, their prime aim was to neutralise all the German coastal batteries, so that the assault troops could land. Thereafter, their task would be to prevent the enemy from moving reinforcements into the area, particularly on the flanks, and to engage specific targets as called for by the army. But the bombardment forces (which mostly came from the west) did not just consist of battleships, cruisers and destroyers. Specialist craft were designed and built for such assaults: landing craft (gun); landing craft (rocket); landing craft (flak) (the Allied forces had adopted the

German term). In all, there were some 46 separate types of specialised landing craft for various functions.

In planning Operation NEPTUNE, the role of the Air Force should not be forgotten. Specifically, the RAF and Fleet Air Arm (operating from Lee-on-the-Solent and Worthy Down) provided spotter aircraft for the bombarding forces, and overall fighter cover for the whole fleet, in addition to the tactical support to the army.

Another aspect of the assault plan was the need for 'balanced loading'. By this is meant the need to ensure that the soldiers arrived with all the necessary equipment for their individual force. In other words, a ship carrying a cargo of motor transport also carried the fuel and the drivers;

if 25-pdr guns travelled in a ship, then that ship also carried the gunners and 25-pdr ammunition. The lesson had been learnt in Norway in 1940, when, in attempting to provide defence for the port of Namsos, under heavy air bombardment, a cargo of AA guns had been sent in one ship (which was equipped for loading and unloading such cargo), while the ammunition had been sent in a ship better fitted for that cargo. The ammunition ship was sunk, so the army received a lot of guns which were unusable. One of the tasks which had to be undertaken by shipyards in the months before D-Day was to make sure that, for example, a ship capable of carrying and handling guns could also carry and handle the ammunition.

In addition, of course, loading plans had to be very carefully drawn up, ship by ship, and inside individual ships, to ensure that cargo was discharged in the order it was needed.

Finally, the planning for NEPTUNE contained an element of deception. To ensure that our forces achieved as much surprise as possible, it was desirable to fool the Germans as to where we were going to land. It was thought unlikely that we would be able to conceal effectively when we were going to land but decoy operations took place right up to the last moment: indeed, the only loss incurred by one of the specialist

A dredger and a jetty under construction at Hayling Island. The Nelson monument is in the background (IWM)

beach survey parties previously mentioned occurred some three-and-a-half weeks before D-Day, when a survey party was captured, but this was up in the Somme area, which helped to give credence to the idea that the Allies intended to land there.

Deception operations continued even after the actual landings began. By spreading confusion among the enemy, these ancillary operations assisted in delaying the commitment of German reserves against the Normandy bridgeheads. They made a valuable contribution to the Allied effort to get established on the mainland.

Landing craft in the Solent (ENHT)

The Build-Up

As has been remarked earlier, the whole operation had to be postponed from May to June, to allow for the construction of sufficient landing craft. Many were built in the USA, particularly the landing ships (tank) (LSTs). These were large ships, of ocean-going size. In the UK, every ship and boatyard was already working at full stretch, building and repairing warships, large and small, steel and wood, and merchant ships to replace the losses in the Battle of the Atlantic and on the convoy routes around the UK. On top of this, it was necessary to modify many ships for their role in Neptune and to increase the rate of building, particularly of small assault craft. The result was that, for

example, landing craft (assault) (LCA) were assembled, literally, in back streets and on improvised hards at the water's edge.

Having planned for the right number of ships (and, in fact, the army had had to accept a reduction in the number of vehicles which were to be landed in the early stages), it was necessary to make provision for loading them. LSTs and the smaller LCTs (landing craft (tank)) could best be loaded by nosing them up to a sloping hard, and then driving the tanks and other vehicles on board – backwards! So hards had to be built specially, and a construction unit was formed and trained at Stokes Bay and set to work to build hards inside Portsmouth harbour and up the coast to the Hamble – the one at Lee-on-the-Solent was

built at that time. In addition, four hards were built inside the docks at Southampton, as well as at Marchwood and on the Beaulieu river.

Another marine service which had to be provided was slipways, on which small craft could be hauled out of the water for repair. It was not sufficient to build landing craft; as will be seen, their inexperienced crews had to be taught to use them and inevitably there were accidents. In any case, grounding a craft, even if done carefully and deliberately, and when the craft has been designed to take the ground, leads to bumps and dents, or worse. So well over a dozen slips were built, not just for landing craft repairs, but for the MTBs and MLs.

In overall charge was the King's Harbour Master in Portsmouth but the individual Port Authorities and their staffs – all civilians – were deeply involved; for example, the Southern Railway, which owned the Port of Southampton, was responsible for laying all the additional moorings in and around the port and up the Itchen. In fact, there were moorings in small creeks all around the Solent. Buoys were laid, and mooring piles driven, in virtually every corner of navigable water around the Solent: landing craft were to be found in Keyhaven, across at Yarmouth and Newtown, in the Beaulieu river and at Ashlett, near Fawley, to name but a few.

Commandos embark on the Hamble
(IWM)

Training

The provision of the ships and craft was only one half of the problem: the other was the provision and training, both general and specialist, of the officers and men who were to man them. The crews for the landing craft were made up largely of very young men who had joined up for the duration of the war. For many, it was their first experience of being in a ship of any kind. Many of their petty officers were relatively inexperienced, as were their officers.

The problem of officers was a crucial

The crew of LCT 2130 on D plus 20 – note the ship's cat! (private collection)

one: throughout the war, the Naval College at Dartmouth (which moved to Eaton Hall, near Chester, in 1942) had continued to train young men as naval officers, and in larger numbers than in peacetime. So too did the Merchant Navy colleges, for the Merchant Navy. But far and away the largest number of young officers were drawn from those who had been in the Royal Naval Volunteer Reserve (RNVR) before the war, or who, after a period on the lower deck as sailors during the war, had been selected for a commission. They were to be found in virtually every ship in the navy, but something like 95% of officers in the landing craft and coastal forces were RNVR.

The demand for junior officers for landing craft was quite out of proportion to the rest of the navy. For example, a battleship might have one officer for every 20 men, with similar proportions in cruisers and destroyers. But in landing craft, it might be one to seven, or even less. As a result, a special training scheme had to be set up to produce the junior officers for landing craft. This was based in Scotland, at Lochailort.

For ratings, the Navy opened a number of shore establishments to train the tens of thousands of young ratings needed by the fleet. H.M.S. *Collingwood*, between Fareham and Lee-on-the-Solent, was opened in

1942 and quickly became one of the largest of all naval establishments. It is a far cry from the 1942 establishment to today's modern complex. The site was marshy and the original camp consisted solely of wooden huts, not just because they could be put up quickly but because the ground would not bear the weight of anything heavier. It was not until the late 1950s that a two-storey building appeared on the site. Having been given their basic naval training, these young men had to be taught to handle their craft. To some extent, it could be said that they had to unlearn a lot of what they had been taught, because a sailor has it dinned into him from an early stage that to hazard your ship by running aground leads to a court-martial and other unpleasant consequences. Yet here they were, being invited to do so deliberately!

The sheltered waters of Langstone Harbour and Chichester Harbour were the site of their basic training. H.M.S. *Northney* was set up on the northern end of Hayling Island and here they learnt the rudiments of seamanship as applied to their unhandy craft and also how to beach and unbeach. Once they were passed out as proficient, they went on to Scotland, where they met up with the army and went on to practice actually embarking and disembarking troops, first as single units and then in groups; by night and by day;

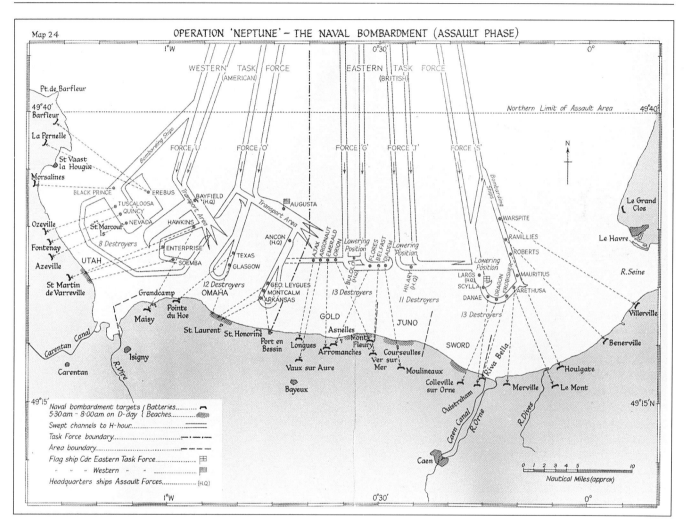

The naval bombardment plan (HMSO)

and with live ammunition being used. Nothing was left to chance. Sailors were even given specific training in looking after soldiers on board the large Landing Ships (Infantry) – stumbling around an unfamiliar ship in the dark, loaded with all your equipment (which seems to have been designed to catch on anything sticking out), could be both awkward and even dangerous. So, in the interests of safety and of speed, it made sense to detail off sailors to help.

LCT(R) loading in Southampton Docks (HJC)

The spirit of the times, and the air of camaraderie is well expressed in the words of a young RN Sub-Lieutenant, who was given command of an LCA:

"When away from the mother ship, the crew camped on board with no facilities except a single bucket for all purposes, and army compo rations.

"My crew consisted first of the coxwain, Leading Seaman Reginald Fulford, a delightful twenty year-old from Stoke-on-Trent, where he returned after the war on completion of nine years' service to become a pottery manager. His firm leadership gained him the nickname 'Der Fuhrer'. Next, the combined sternsheetsman, Lewis gunner and 2-inch mortar crew was nineteen year-old A.B. 'Snakey' Walsh. He was a fine athlete and swimmer, and an accomplished signwriter who emblazoned the craft with a magnificent picture of Father Neptune on his plunging steed and also our chosen name for the LCA – Grey Dawn. He was a quietly spoken man, whose worst oath when things went badly wrong was 'Horror of Horrors'.

"The final member of the team was a dear old greybeard stoker named Tapner, in his mid thirties and married with a baby daughter. In civil life he was a London ambulance driver. His engine-room with its twin Ford V8 petrol engines would have done justice to a millionaire's yacht or a C-in-C's barge – copper pipe-work burnished, bulkheads white enamelled and decks holystoned."

Another naval task was control of the beaches: that is, to ensure that the right craft came in at the right time, in the right place; to ensure that the army were there to take charge of what was unloaded, and that the beached craft was then refloated and sent back to England for more, as soon as possible. The Beachmaster (a Captain, RN) and his team were also responsible for ensuring that the army cleared the stores dumped as soon as possible, so that the beach did not get too congested, thus further hindering

movement, and presenting the enemy's artillery with a really worthwhile target.

There was one more major training task: to exercise the bombarding ships in the specialist shore bombardment techniques, in particular co-operation with the army and the spotters, both on land and in the air. Most of this took place in north-west Scotland. (Cape Wrath has probably had a greater weight of ammunition expended on it than was dropped on London during the blitz. It is still used for live firings today.)

The naval bombardment was seen as being a vital part of the assault. Its task was three-fold: before H-Hour, the enemy's shore batteries had to be neutralised, so that the assault forces could reach their beaches unmolested. The timing of this phase was crucial. It was not expected that the enemy's artillery would be destroyed: many of the batteries were protected by reinforced concrete many metres thick, which would be affected by only the largest of naval artillery. But it was expected that the use of armour-piercing shells would cause much disruption to the working and control and ammunition supply, by causing the guns' crews to seek shelter. If this could be done while the assault craft were making their run in, the necessary neutralisation would be achieved: but it couldn't

be started too early, or else the enemy would receive advance warning of the points at which the assault was to be made.

The second phase of the bombardment followed immediately after the first. Fire was to be concentrated on the enemy's lesser defences – pillboxes, machine-gun posts, anti-tank defences and the like. From the foregoing, it will be seen how vital was accurate reconnaissance. The positions of batteries, redoubts and so on had to be known, as far as possible, before D-Day.

The final phase was known as 'drenching fire'. In this phase, the beaches and the area immediately behind them were saturated with shellfire, with the aim of preventing, literally, any single defender from offering any defence at all. For this phase the destroyers and the specialist landing craft were used. One of the most effective was the LCT(R), each of which discharged a ripple of 800 to 1000 rockets whose total firepower was equivalent to a single broadside from 150 destroyers. These craft were fearsomely awful, in the proper sense of the word, when they fired their 'broadside'. Since the rocket tubes were fixed, aiming was achieved by pointing the ship at the target. The heat generated was terrific, and despite the decks being sprayed with water, they became distorted. No-one could remain on deck, and the

King George VI transfers from H.M.S. Scylla to ML 529, 24th May 1944 (IWM)

Captain conned the ship from a blast- and heat-proof hutch at the stern.

The total number of ships allocated to bombardment was 31 battleships, monitors and cruisers, plus 57 destroyers and 90 bombardment landing craft. On 6th June, their impact on the enemy was shattering.

Final Preparations

On 26th April, 1944, Admiral Ramsay moved into Southwick House with his staff. Inside the house, the drawing room was converted into the Operations Room, with a map of the eastern half of the English Channel covering one wall. (This map is still in the same position.) On this were marked the beaches, the routes, the swept channels, etc., and, for security reasons, only the immediate staffs of the Cs-in-C and the WRNS plotters were allowed in there. The secret of the invasion was also known to one other person in the Portsmouth area – the dockyard carpenter who had erected the wall map, who for six weeks was entrusted with one of the most momentous secrets of the war.

The invasion was to be a combined operation in every sense of the word. British ships carried American soldiers and *vice versa*. British warships operated under American command and *vice versa*. Having worked up as individual units and then as groups, there was a final dress rehearsal, Operation FABIUS, between 2nd and 6th May. Forces S and J carried out their landings on beaches in West Sussex, while Force G landed on Hayling. Forces O and U landed on Slapton Sands, in Devon, in two separate exercises, during one of which German E-boats came across the force and sank two LCTs and damaged a third, with the loss of 638 men.

It was not until 1st May that the date and time of D-Day and H-Hour were finally settled. The requirements were complex: the night before had to be moonlit, for the paratroops. The first landings had to be made within a period from 12 minutes before, to 90 minutes after, sunrise, and had to be three to four hours before high water. There were only two possible periods in the month when this combination of circumstances prevailed, 5 – 7th and 18 – 20th June. The earlier period was favoured: delay could only increase the risk that the Germans would tumble to the fact that the invasion was about to be launched, and the troops would 'go off the boil'. Because of the way the tide progresses up the Channel, the time of high water got progressively later from west to east: and so too did H-Hour. On UTAH and OMAHA beaches it was 0630 hours: on GOLD beach it was 0725 hours: on

JUNO, it was 0735 – 0745 hours, while on SWORD, although the most easterly, it was 0725 hours.

Throughout May, commanders got to know the forces under their command. Captain G.V.M. Dolphin, Royal Navy, who was to command the third section of Force G, and then to become the Naval beach-master on GOLD Beach, described how he was appointed only three weeks before D-Day. He was based at Exbury House, which had become H.M.S. *Mastodon*, and found himself in command of about 40 Landing Craft Infantry (Large) (LCI(L)), plus LCI(S)s, LCMs (M for Mechanised), Landing Barge (Kitchen) (LBK), LBE (E for Emergency Repair). The LCIs, both large and small, could make about 12 knots, but the LCMs and the barges could only make about 5 – 6 knots. The LCI(L)s each carried 200 fully-equipped troops, who could be disembarked in five minutes, by means of two ramps, lowered from each side of the ship. The LCI(S)s carried 96 troops. This force was to carry the two reserve brigades of the 50th Division. One problem he discovered was that many of the captains of the LCIs were not used to navigating in a tideway, having come from the virtually tideless Mediterranean. He had to explain that, if they were to keep within the swept channels and at the same time maintain station on their next ahead, they are going to

have to learn, fast, the art of keeping station on a line of bearing. When they realised that the consequences of not so doing could well be the explosion of a mine underneath, they learned – and on D-Day their station keeping was excellent.

Another exercise which Captain Dolphin insisted on being practised was the unloading of the big LSTs. The landing of the support armour for the infantry was vital and, although the LSTs were configured for beaching, it had been decreed that they should not do so, at least, not when they had a full load of tanks, lest they should break their backs.

The method of unloading was for the LST to open its bow doors, and for a 'Rhino' ferry (a long, very low, pontoon, powered by outboard motors) to nose up to the LST; the tanks would then drive on to the 'Rhino', which would then beach itself. The whole operation was fairly hair-raising, but worked in the Solent. Finally, he held a parade in one of the transit sheds in Southampton Docks, so that, at the least, all the men in GG3, some 2,000 British, American, Canadian and French, knew who it was commanding them: this was followed by a service. Much the same routine was followed in all the landing forces.

On 24th May, HM King George VI inspected the units of the fleet. He embarked in C-in-C Portsmouth's barge at Exbury pier, and inspected all the craft in the minor anchorages in the west Solent, and then embarked in an ML off Cowes to travel down to Spithead.

The orders for OVERLORD were opened on 25th May, and D-Day (then 5th June) and the various H-Hours were promulgated to all concerned. From that time, all personnel were 'sealed' in their ships or camps. On 31st May, loading commenced and was completed by 3rd June, without any interference by the enemy.

Delay

The weather was always going to be a critical factor in the landings: if it were too rough, the crossing might take longer than planned, with the result that the landings might be late but, most importantly, the assault craft might be swamped, or broach to on the beach, or suffer from any of the other 'dangers of the sea', without regard to 'the violence of the enemy'. The last fortnight of May had seen excellent weather but at the beginning of June it started to deteriorate.

As described earlier (Chapter 3), this deterioration forced a postponement of the date for D-Day, but this decision could not be taken until many of the convoys had already left British ports. All these convoys were successfully turned back, except for one from Devon which

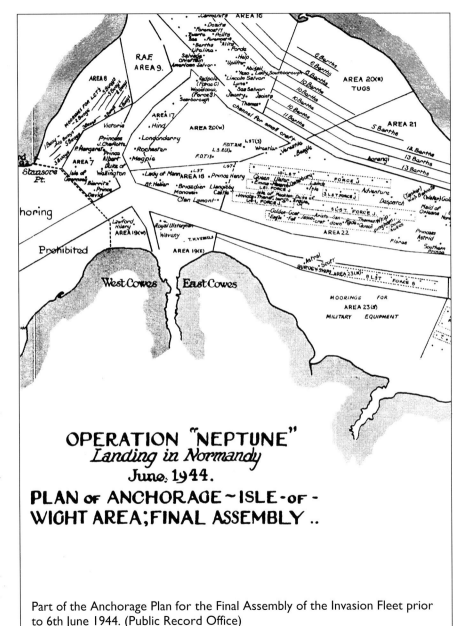

OPERATION "NEPTUNE"
Landing in Normandy
June, 1944.
PLAN of ANCHORAGE ~ ISLE - of - WIGHT AREA; FINAL ASSEMBLY ..

Part of the Anchorage Plan for the Final Assembly of the Invasion Fleet prior to 6th June 1944. (Public Record Office)

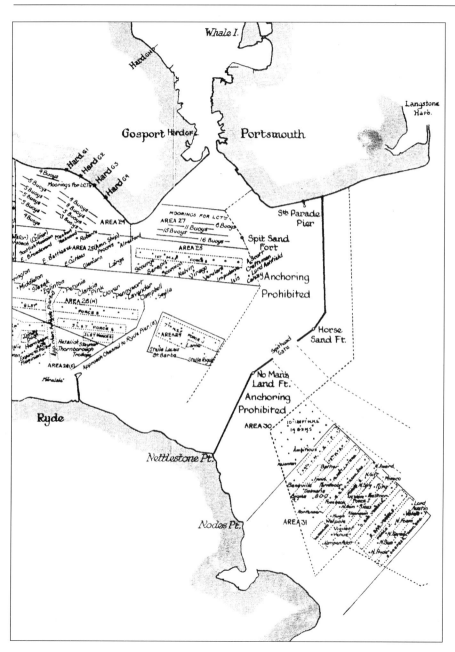

did not receive the signal. It was finally found and turned back by a Walrus amphibian from RNAS Lee-on-the-Solent. Luck had been with them, because, having effectively got ahead of their mine-sweepers (which had delayed their own operations), these latter subsequently found mines right in the track of the convoy. Although most of these were swiftly swept, one of them claimed the first victim of Operation NEPTUNE, the mine-sweeper U.S.S. *Osprey*, on 5th June.

One other part of the invasion forces had an uncomfortable wait during the period of postponement. Operation Gambit required two midget submarines, X-20 and X-23 to sail from H.M.S. *Dolphin* at Gosport on Friday 2nd June. They were escorted by trawlers about one-third of the way across and then made their way submerged to positions about one mile off Ouistreham at the eastern end of SWORD beach. Their job was to surface on the morning of D-Day, to show lights and markers indicating the limits of the beaches and in particular where the amphibious tanks could come ashore. Having arrived at dawn on the morning of 4th June, they checked their positions and then returned to the bottom again until tea time, when they checked their position again and returned to the bottom once more. Just before midnight, they surfaced, ran inshore to their final position and anchored. But two hours later, they received the postponement signal, and so, being too close to the shore for comfort, retired a mile or so further out to sea. The postponement meant that they had to stay submerged throughout 5th June, in conditions of severe discomfort, with five men in a cabin 5 ft 8 ins in diameter by 5 ft long.

D-DAY

Command and Control

It had originally been proposed that Admiral Ramsay would take command of the Allied naval forces afloat, controlling the naval operations from a suitable flagship. But the complexity of the operation soon made it clear that the Commander-in-Chief could not exercise tactical command afloat, as well as managing the flow of shipping across the Channel. Accordingly, Rear-Admiral Sir Philip Vian, a most distinguished fighting Admiral, who had had experience of command of a landing force during the invasion of Sicily, was appointed to command the British Naval Task Force. And the expansion of the scope of the invasion to a five-division front, together with the introduction of an American Task Force, led to a further split, with Rear Admiral Alan

Kirk taking command of the Western Task Force, while Admiral Vian commanded the Eastern. These Task Forces were not split on 'nationalist' lines: RN, Free French and Dutch ships served under Admiral Kirk, while Admiral Vian's force contained British, Polish, Dutch, Free French, Norwegian, Greek and US ships. So far as this narrative is concerned, covering the association of the County of Hampshire with the landings, the emphasis will be on the happenings on the British and Canadian beaches, which were the concern of the Eastern Task Force.

Navigation

It is not unfair to say that many of the minor landing craft were commanded by men who were not very skilled in navigation. Nor were they fitted with the necessary equipment. And yet accurate navigation was vital. Each craft had a specified place to go to: while even more necessary was the need to keep within the swept channels. The sweeping of these channels had to be carried out with the utmost accuracy.

Fortunately, in October 1941, the Admiralty had become aware of the potential of an experimental navigation system, being developed by the Decca company and had pressed ahead with its development. This system, which works by comparing

the phase shifts of radio signals received from stations in known, fixed, positions, produced fixes (ie, it gives the navigator his measured position) to within a 10-yard accuracy. [The author can vouch for this – in an ML proceeding through the Downs, off east Kent, on a dark night, he took a Decca fix, and came up on to the bridge remarking, 'That unlit buoy ought to be here or hereabouts'. At which precise moment the buoy went bumping down the ML's side.] The Decca system, or QM as it was then known, was made available to the senior ships of all the minesweeping flotillas plus half a dozen other of the lead ships of the individual forces.

As has been described above, the submarines X-20 and X-23 had spent an uncomfortable day on the seabed off Ouistreham. (The Captain of X-23 noted that there was even a light showing at the mouth of the Orne canal.) The crew had to rely on replenishing their oxygen from cylinders which had been recovered from crashed German aircraft – they were the only ones which could be found which were light enough. (It may also be remarked that X-23 had been built in Chesterfield – not a place that one would expect to be associated with shipbuilding but an example of how all and every facility which could be turned to account was used in the war.) At 0445 hours on the morning of 6th June, they surfaced, and set up their 18 ft high masts, and started flashing their signals 20 minutes later, replacing the light with a large flag when there was sufficient light. They also operated a sonar set, whose pulses could be picked up by the lead ships of the approaching convoys. Two hours later, with the first troops ashore, they slipped their cable, being too exhausted to weigh it, and reported to the HQ ship, H.M.S. *Largs*. Later, they made their way back to Gosport and H.M.S. *Dolphin*, where they received a traditional submariners' welcome for boats returning from a successful mission, though the Captain of X-23, nearly 50 years after the event, wrote, 'We were especially relieved to return safely, as we had looked up the definition of our code word Gambit in the dictionary, and it was defined as 'the pawn you throw away before a big move in chess.' (An X-craft can still be seen in the RN Submarine Museum at Gosport.)

At the western end, where the water was shallower, the limits of the beaches were marked by two Harbour Defence MLs, nos. 1383 and 1387. These two were also fitted with the QM navigation system, and made their way over to France silently in the early hours of the morning of 6th June, anchoring at the north end of OMAHA beach. (ML 1387 is still afloat, in private hands.)

A US Liberty ship sunk by a mine off Normandy at 0700 hours on D plus 18 (private collection)

Minesweeping

The thrust and counter-thrust of mine-versus-mine counter-measures is one of the less known stories of the war – and much of the development of British mines took place at West Leigh House, near Havant. By this stage of the war, mines were of many types, not merely the 'traditional' round moored mine with horns, which was buoyant and was laid with a sinker attached, and which exploded when a ship hit it.

All through 5th June, 10 flotillas of fleet minesweepers swept the 10 channels of 'the spout' from Area Z southwards, each channel being marked, as it was swept, by special buoy-laying trawlers. The 14th Minesweeping Flotilla came within sight of the French coast at 1940 that evening, and the 16th Flotilla an hour later. But, for a reason that has never been satisfactorily explained, the Germans did not react. Having swept the path across the Channel (in doing so, a total of 29 mines were swept), the sweepers then had to sweep out an area parallel to the shore for the transports to anchor to land their assault craft. And then

H.M.S. Emerald bombarding German coastal batteries on the afternoon of D-Day. Taken from LCT 2130, one mile off the mouth of the River Vire (private collection)

they had to sweep the areas for the bombarding ships.

Altogether, the minesweepers swept 292 mines between 6th and 30th June, for the loss of six warships and three others, with 18 warships and three others damaged.

Bombardment

The minesweepers had swept separate lanes for the bombarding ships in the vicinity of the beaches. In the eastern area, during the initial phase, 15 identified batteries were engaged by 16 ships mounting guns 5.25 ins (133 mm) in calibre up to 15 ins (380 mm), plus a further 37 destroyers. This whole bombardment force was under the command of Rear-Admiral Patterson, who was in turn responsible to Rear-Admiral Vian. Fire was opened at 0530

hours, and continued until the targets had been neutralised: the times varied, depending on the accuracy of the fire, and the resistance (or resilience) of the defenders. In fact, the task had been made more difficult, because many of the enemy batteries were not where they were expected to be. After the massive pre-D-Day air strikes, the Germans had moved many of their guns and so the initial bombardments and air strikes merely damaged abandoned gun emplacements: but at the same time, their new positions were only half-completed, and were less effective when the assault did come. Spotting for the ships' fire was carried out by Seafires of 808, 885 and 886 Squadrons, operating from Lee-on-the-Solent .

It was just at the start of the bombardment that the Germans made their only surface ship attack on the

invasion fleet on that day but it is not unfair to say that this was more of an accident than a planned counter-attack. The Allied plan had called for dummy landings and feint attacks to be made elsewhere along the French coast: small ships towing barrage balloons appeared on German radar screens as convoys on the move in the Dover Straits, and a smoke screen in the Baie de la Seine concealed what was happening, to such good effect that the Germans were not convinced that the real attack was being launched on Normandy. A force of torpedo boats were sent out from Le Havre to investigate and on emerging from the smoke screen found themselves in the middle of Admiral Patterson's bombarding ships. The Germans fired a salvo of 18 torpedoes, and achieved one hit on the Norwegian destroyer Svenner, which sank, fortunately with little loss of life.

After the initial landings and as the army enlarged its beachheads the nature of the naval gunfire support changed. From bombarding pre-determined targets, ships turned to responding to calls for fire from the artillery observers ashore. The results were summarised by Admiral Ramsay, in his report, 'By common consent, the shooting was uniformly good and it is considered that the initial advances of our armies were helped in no small measure by the naval supporting fire.' When the German sources became available after the war, it was found that their war diary for 20th June recorded, 'It is generally accepted that the intended offensive of the German Army has no chance of success unless the exceedingly effective shelling by enemy naval guns of our own land units can be prevented. The German Navy is not capable of making an attack. The Luftwaffe which is numerically just as inferior also refuses to attack naval targets by day. As the battleships move away from the coastal area at night there appears to be no solution.'

Across the Channel

For Captain Dolphin, 'the passage over to Far Shore was uneventful'. But for another Reserve officer, it was rather different. He was in command of a landing barge flotilla, which sailed from the Solent on D-Day minus 1.

"We had a special cargo and were already loaded. We were carrying high-grade 100-octane to refuel the assault craft after their first run in. From D until D+4, our Flotilla was to keep the entire Naval Assault Force off our beachhead supplied with petrol and diesel – everything and anything from LCAs up to destroyers. We expected to be busy.

"We had always regarded the barges as silly trundling old things –

Across the Channel: an LCT carrying US troops heads for Normandy (private collection)

definitely the lowest form of marine life. After all, they were only converted Thames lighters which had never been designed to go to sea. But now, looking down the trots of buoys at the hundreds of barges stretching away up the estuary, we felt quite pleased with them. Singly they were rather stupid but collectively they acquired a sort of clumsy strength.

"..... and at three that afternoon the Signal went up 'Prepare to Weigh'. Immediately, hundreds of engines sprang into life and the mighty roar they made seemed to express our relief at getting going at last. As barge after barge switched on its

engines all down that long line, the roar increased to a fury of sound that must have been heard for miles inland.

"..... We slipped from the buoy and started down the estuary. One after the other the barges peeled off from their moorings and took up station astern of us according to pre-arranged order. I had never seen so many under way at one time – they stretched away, an ensign fluttering from each, as far as the eye could see. And still they kept coming, their engines thundering and roaring. It took the convoy a full hour to get clear of the estuary. We felt proud of the barges that day.

"As we approached the rendezvous point a couple of hours later, we fairly gaped – for there ahead of us was surely assembled the greatest mass of shipping ever seen. And this was only one of scores of assembly points all round the coasts of Britain. Troop transports, great carriers, ships and craft of every size and description were converging from every direction.

"Four Hunt-class destroyers came belting out of the Solent, picking their way through hundreds of craft scattered around. Then they turned in succession to port, all heeling over together in magnificent station-keeping. A light cruiser shot past us at full speed on her way to meet a convoy which was still just a forest of masts and funnels on the horizon.

"The general excitement was so great that I only now fully registered one fact – that the sea was rough. This meant little to real ships with a keel but it meant a whole lot to flat-bottomed barges. And it was blowing up, too. We had never been allowed to exercise in more than Force 4 and were now rolling around in Force 5 or 6.

"One of our escorting MLs rolled up and signalled us to follow. Well, this was it. All the ships were still at anchor but we had to start before them because of our slow speed. Like children being packed off to bed early while the grown-ups sat around talking, we threaded our way through the maze of shipping close on the heels of our nanny, the ML.

"Our station keeping was lousy. It was impossible for barges to keep station in that sea. Those long months we had spent practising cruising dispositions were no use to us that day. The barges just lurched and rolled drunkenly in the waves and followed the leaders as best they could. Remembering those Hunt-class destroyers I reflected disgustedly that this was an awfully undignified way to go to the second front.

"Leading our Flotilla was an armed trawler whose duty it was to take in tow any barge that might break down. It is recorded that the trawler skipper, who had never seen one of our barges before that afternoon, kept looking back from his bridge with a mixture of incredulity and pity and muttering repeatedly 'the poor ....' It was twilight now, and as the Channel coast receded into the distance, I reflected that when I next stepped ashore it would be on to a French beach.

"We were taking a sweeping zig-zag course so as not to disclose our eventual destination to the enemy reconnaissance craft. As darkness came down, the ML circled round, calling us through her loudhailer to keep closed up.

"Very soon after dark came what we had been expecting. On our starboard beam a cluster of star-shells went up. E-boats! Almost immediately there followed the streams of red tracer bullets, describing their graceful leisurely arcs.

"It's amazing how a flare at sea on a dark night makes you feel naked and exposed. We had our orders: only to open fire if directly attacked so as not to give away our position. The escort was to deal primarily with attackers. Our gun crews were closed up and all life-belts inflated. I thought of our cargo tanks carrying twelve thousand gallons of 100-octane. It would only require one armour-piercing bullet .....

"The Battle lasted half an hour. The trawler's bridge got hit, and so did a few barges (but not, thank the Lord, in the fuel tanks). The casualties weren't heavy. The E-boats cleared off – no doubt they had spotted better game. The barges must have been a very difficult target in that sea as they sat very low in the water and were hidden by waves half the time.

"In the darknesss we were still lurching and wallowing in the heavy sea. A few were straggling, but somehow that amazing convoy kept on its course. (I made a mental note. First-class on the boat when visiting France after the war.)

"The sea grew rougher. Two hours later the trawlers had their hands full, towing at least three barges apiece. Other barges were straggling badly, and the ML kept circling round and exhorting them to keep closed up. They kept ploughing on through it, gunwales awash – indeed submerged most of the time. ('A fine bloody time to hold a Second Front', I reflected.) Now two barges reported that they were shipping water faster than they could pump it out and were sinking. The Squadron Commander's yacht came alongside them and picked the crews off. It was a magnificent piece of seamanship in that heavy sea. Compared with the heavy plunging barges, the yacht was as frail as a cockle-shell and a knock from them would have holed and sunk her instantly.

"The dawn light revealed some mines floating around. It also revealed that three of the stragglers were missing. Whether they filled up and sank, or got picked off by E-boats, or struck mines, we don't know. Those three barges were never seen or heard of again.

"The heavy weather had reduced our already slow speed. Our progress was in striking contrast to the great fleets of aircraft passing overhead. (As a movie-man, my sense of presentation was outraged that the barges should shuffle and lurch at Hitler's Atlantic Wall – instead of charging at it nobly like those Hunt-class destroyers!)

"When we reached the assault area, that mass of shipping that had left England so long after us was already there. We travelled along the coast to our beachhead amid an inferno of noise. Battleships of the Home Fleet were pounding hell out of the coast batteries, mines were going up all round us, shells rained down.

"But the sea had calmed and the sun was out, and we thanked the Lord for being delivered from the nightmare voyage amidst the perils of the sea into the peace and security of the battle area."

Troops wade ashore from an RN LCI(L) (IWM)

The Assault Landing

The three Hampshire forces, G, J and S, were due to land almost simultaneously, between 0725 hours and 0745 hours. Force G, consisting of 243 ships, reached its lowering position at 0455 hours. This was nearly seven miles off the beaches and, as Admiral Vian later wrote,

the weather 'was unexpectedly severe for the launching of an operation of this type'. The lowering position was chosen to be relatively out of range of the enemy defences and to allow sufficient sea-room for the assault craft to form up before reaching the beaches. The Large and Medium Landing Ships (Infantry) lowered their quota of LCAs, which set off for the shore in formation, accompanied by their support craft. The troops had an uncomfortable ride, lasting about one-and-a-quarter hours, and many were sea-sick. The earliest craft touched down some seven-and-a-half minutes before H-Hour. These were the LCTs (AVRE), which carried the Royal Engineer demolition parties, whose job it was to dismantle the beach obstacles. These turned out to be more numerous than had been expected and so, when the LCAs brought the first wave of assault troops in, some were damaged and the rough sea caused a number to broach to on the beach, hindering later forces. But, by and large, GOLD beach operations went according to plan and to schedule. Captain Dolphin described it thus:

"Once the Reserve Brigades had been put ashore I put on my other 'hat' of Naval Officer in Charge Gold and the Sub-Area Commander [his Army opposite number] and I plus our own operational staffs landed but not dry-shod! – there were two- to three-foot waves. The time was about 0830 hours, and it was half-tide. There was a bit of sniping going on, but the main thing was the beach obstacles. These were iron posts driven into the sand with land mines secured to the top of them. The demolition parties were busy blowing them up as the beach had to be cleared by the next high tide when the build-up was to start.

"..... we went on a 'recce' to select an operational HQ. .....there was a most convenient two-storied house, which provided a perfect view of the beaches..... We took it over...... Our Air Force had blown the roof off the house, so we covered it with a tarpaulin. Soon we had a flagstaff with a large White Ensign flying set up in front of the house on a grass plot which we surrounded with stones painted white – et voila! Le QUARTERDECK!"

By 2100 hours that night, Arromanches had been taken, the site for one of the MULBERRY harbours: and early the next day, Royal Marine Commandos captured Port-en-Bessin, a small port at the western end of GOLD beach.

Force J consisted of 187 ships, and Force S, 285 ships. Force S had its bombarding force specially strengthened by the inclusion of H.M.S. *Warspite*, H.M.S. *Ramillies* and the monitor H.M.S. *Roberts*. These ships mounted 15-ins guns and were given the heavy German batteries at Le Havre as their targets.

Of course, it was inevitable that not every craft of each group reached its exact destination at precisely the right time but nonetheless it was with some satisfaction that Admiral Ramsay could write in his report of the operation that, 'the outstanding fact was that despite the unfavourable weather, in every main essential the plan was carried out as written'.

The Build-Up

The next phase of Operation NEPTUNE consisted of a meticulously planned build-up of troops and supplies – and in this phase the port of Southampton played the major part. To ensure a smooth flow of supplies to the Allied armies, two organisations had been set up as part of NEPTUNE – the Build-Up Control Organisation (BUCO) and the Turn-Round Control Organisation (TURCO). Their overall aim was to make the most economic use of the available shipping. BUCO dealt with the more general co-ordination of shipping with the needs of the military, while TURCO did the detailed routeing of individual ships to ports and berths where cargoes were waiting.

Admiral Ramsay's plan had been to ensure that the maximum amount of supplies were landed in the first three days: thereafter, there was to be a three-day cycle of convoys, to produce a smooth flow of men and stores through the beaches. Within this plan, the aim was that the LSTs and LCTs should, so far as possible, use the same berths each time they came into port.

Traffic was not all one way: inevitably there were casualties to be brought home, and German prisoners as well. Petty Officer George Drewett had spent the early years of the war in H.M.S. *Brocklesby*, operating out of Portsmouth, but just before D-Day he had come back to Portsmouth after duty in the Mediterranean. He was in the RN Barracks, and two days after D-Day was detailed off to form part of a scratch crew for a converted LCT, which was to bring back casualties from the beaches. They made three trips in all, anchoring off the beaches, while the casualties were ferried out in smaller craft. They made their passages unescorted, but were not attacked, although they did not wear a Red Cross like the hospital ships. Each time, they brought their precious cargo back to the South Railway Jetty in Portsmouth, to be transferred to ambulances to take the wounded to hospitals in the area.

In Normandy, the beaches were still exposed to a moderate sea and casualties among the landing craft were high. It was therefore necessary to clear the beaches of obstacles as soon as possible and to provide shelter for the small craft. On D-Day plus 1, the GOOSEBERRIES started to arrive – old warships which were to be scuttled to form breakwaters. They at once made a difference, and the landing of men, equipment and stores went on apace. In the first week, on average there arrived off the beaches each day:

25 cargo ships (mostly 'Liberty' or 'Victory' ships); 38 coasters; 9 troop-ships; 40 LSTs; 75 LCTs; 20 LCI(L)s

Supplying the advance: Allied craft in a French harbour, possibly Port-en-Bessin (private collection)

On GOLD beach, where the unloading of armour was going very slowly, Captain Dolphin had taken a decision to beach the LSTs, instead of using the Rhino ferries. Despite the planners' fears for the crafts' safety, this was done, with no ill-effects, and unloading of the vital tanks proceeded according to schedule.

Back in the Solent, the waters were almost as crowded as they had been immediately before D-Day. The Shell-Mex and BP terminal at Hamble had had its jetty extended shortly before D-Day, and this became the loading point for the tankers which kept the armies supplied with fuel in the weeks before PLUTO became operational. One of Hamble's greatest achievements was on 5th June, when no fewer than 212 ships of all sizes topped up their bunker supplies in the 24 hours before D-Day.

Portsmouth now reverted largely to being an operational Naval

Dockyard and base. But Southampton became the major port in the United Kingdom for supplies for the United States forces in Europe, with ships arriving from the United States, as well as ships being loaded and despatched to France. All these were handled by the 14th Major Port Unit of the US Transportation Corps, working with the Southern Railway's port staff. The figures speak for themselves, to show the magnitude of their work. In the 15 weeks following D-Day, the port had a throughput of 1,002,955 tons of cargo, which was about the same as the whole amount handled in 1939. On one day, 21st July, 75 ships were loaded for France, with 10,603 tons of cargo and some 20,000 men. It is a measure of how cargo handling has changed to observe that Southampton can still handle up to 10,000 tons of cargo per day – but now it goes in one large container ship!

Most of this cargo went to the MULBERRY harbours which were being established off Arromanches in the British/Canadian sector, and St Laurent in the American. In addition, the little harbour of Port-en-Bessin provided an additional bonus by being able to handle up to 1,000 tons of stores per day, while Courseulle had also been taken, and was making a small contribution.

The British MULBERRY was under the command of Captain Petrie, Royal Navy, who had won a DSO and bar in the First World War, and had retired to farm in South Africa. His 'flagship' was the old cruiser H.M.S. *Despatch*, which had been hauled back from the breaker's torch in a near-derelict state, with no armament and no stores. But she sailed on time, with an armament (not recorded in *Janes Fighting Ships*, that bible of ship details) 'borrowed' from the army, manned by soldiers, and with an army Major as her Gunnery Officer!

Holding the Ring

While the Merchant Navies, and landing craft were building up the armies' supplies, the other Allied navies were holding the ring. Operations to keep German forces out of the beach areas extended the whole length of the Channel, as German U-boats from the Biscay ports and small craft from the Boulogne area attempted to disrupt the Allies' build-up. But the main brunt of the fighting was on the flanks of the beaches, particularly at the eastern end, where the 'Trout' line was established: Landing Craft (Flak) and (Gun), MLs and destroyers all formed part of a combined static and patrolling defence system. There were many actions fought, which might be classified as 'small', but to the men who were involved they were every bit as hot as any other great battle. The Germans attempted to break through using their E-boats and larger torpedo boats, and they introduced their 'Biber' one man submarines – basically one torpedo being 'ridden' by a diver, with a second torpedo slung underneath. Nearer England, battles were fought between convoy escorts and E-boats from Cherbourg, which resulted in losses on both sides: the Germans on one occasion torpedoing and sinking one of the great PHOENIX caissons. And throughout this, the Allied minesweepers went about their hazardous work, rendered all the more dangerous because the Germans at last made use of their 'Oyster' pressure mine, dropping it from aircraft as well as from E-boats and other craft.

The Great Gale

By D-Day plus 13, the beachheads were secure, and the build-up was going well. His Majesty the King had paid a visit to JUNO beach, crossing from Portsmouth in the cruiser H.M.S. *Arethusa* on 16th June. But on 19th June, there blew up a gale of unparalleled intensity. The uncompleted MULBERRY off St Laurent was so badly damaged as to be not worth repairing, while the Arromanches one was also badly affected. For example, in the lull before the storm some two-and-a-half miles of WHALE roadway, to

H.M.S. Arethusa covers the invasion fleet (ENHT)

connect the pierheads to the shore, was sailed across the Channel successfully, only to be sunk during the storm.

The beaches were piled with wreckage – and this is not an exaggeration; there were some 800 vessels stranded, ranging from small LCAs to LSTs and coasters. Of these,

about 600 were repaired and refloated by the next spring tide on 8th July, while 100 more were refloated a fortnight later. In the first 30 days after D-Day, no fewer than 153 ships and craft were sunk by the weather, and 437 damaged. Out of 650 LCTs available to Admiral Ramsay, a total of 320 were put out of action, to a greater or lesser degree. However, the repair parties from H.M.S. *Adventure* and H.M.S. *Albatross* patched up the craft, so badly needed to maintain the flow of stores, so that they could limp back to the dockyard in Portsmouth and the other yards between Weymouth and Newhaven.

As a result, the build-up was disrupted: in the 12 days to 18th June, 622,000 men were landed in France: in the next 12 days, only 240,000 were landed. In the first 12 days, 96,000 vehicles and 217,500 tons of stores were landed: in the next 12 days, the totals were 62,000 vehicles and 283,000 tons. It was estimated that 20,000 vehicles and 140,000 tons of stores were not delivered on schedule: ammunition stocks ran dangerously low, and the Allied offensive was delayed, while General Rommel was able to build up his defences.

The first PLUTO pipeline was hauled ashore on 25th June. By 3rd July other pipelines had been completed, giving a capacity of 8,000 tons of fuel per day. Thereafter, the build-up went smoothly, although the Germans continued to try to disrupt the flow of supplies until Le Havre was taken at the beginning of September.

Conclusion

The beginning of July marked the effective end of Operation NEPTUNE, with the disbandment of the command organisation. The beaches were closed at the end of July, Captain Dolphin recording 'We had a monumental party at our esta-minet in La Rivière, and off we went home.' Admiral Ramsay remained as Allied Naval Commander Expeditionary Forces and moved his Headquarters to France from Southwick House, on 7th September.

It had been a most colossal undertaking. Mere figures cannot express its immensity, but changes in the nature of warfare in the last half-century suggest that the world will not see an operation of this scale again – and well for the world that we should not. But Hampshire remains as the springboard from which England's armies have continued to go overseas. The Falklands campaign was almost totally launched from Southampton, Marchwood and Portsmouth, while the more recent Gulf war saw Southampton once again the base from which most of the army's stores and equipment were despatched.

The aftermath of the 'great gale': LCT 1120 beached (private collection)

CHAPTER FIVE

THE PEOPLE OF HAMPSHIRE AND D-DAY

Lesley Burton

During the early years of the war, the life of the people of Hampshire was essentially little different from that of the rest of the nation. Hampshire had played its part in preparing the troops sent to France in 1939 and 1940 and then in receiving them back again after Dunkirk. Hampshire had been a front-line county during the Battle of Britain and subsequently in the attempts to defend Britain against the night blitzes which followed in 1940, 1941 and 1942. And its people shared, particularly, in the personal tragedies associated with the blitz: the two main cities, Southampton and Portsmouth, lost a total of 1,630 dead with 4,743 seriously injured. A third of the housing stock in Portsmouth was destroyed. Even after the worst of the air raids was over, the economic importance of the county kept it in the forefront, both through the exertions of its citizens in turning its industries to meet the demands of war, and because of its geographical location which made it a centre for the increasing military, air and naval activity aimed at enemy forces in occupied France. Pressure was kept up from Hampshire airfields, naval

Ophelia Snodkins loved to ride
On the crown of the road instead of the side.
No signal she gave as she swerved to the right,
So a sprightly young life met its end that night.
Let Ophelia's ghost be a warning to you
If you wish to live to a hundred and two.

LOOK OUT IN THE BLACK-OUT

Perils of the Hampshire black-out, 1944 (HC 18/3/44)

forces based in the county's ports harried German trade and protected our own, and occasional amphibious operations were launched from Hampshire, such as the Dieppe raid.

By 1943, the air raids were mercifully less frequent and apart from the many wartime restrictions, everyday life was returning to something approaching normality. In the towns, theatres were opening, the big bands played to large and enthusiastic audiences of off-duty workers and servicemen, and the county's parish halls and ballrooms resounded to the popular tunes of the period and to the jive and jitterbug. But the wartime restrictions still bore hard on a population increasingly tired after four years of war.

The need to keep the black-out was a tiresome additional chore as well as an unwelcome reminder of the possibility of further air raids but it was also a danger in itself and, while the number of accidents caused by it had decreased since its first introduction, official injunctions to be cautious still continued, some couched in that rather pompous and self-consciously humorous style which now seems characteristic of the period.

Food, of course, was strictly rationed. The getting and growing of food to supplement the sparse wartime diet was everyone's constant preoccupation. It was pursued nowhere more zealously than in the villages of Hampshire. People were urged to dig over their flowerbeds, plough their playing fields and plunder the hedgerows for the war effort. The Women's Institutes did wonders and Netley Marsh Women's Institute is probably typical of many. In 1943 they proudly announced a total production of 588½ lbs of jam and 122 lbs of chutney. School children were recruited in the food drive. The village of Hordle boasted a Youth Service Squad which was mobilised to collect blackberries, nettles and rosehips and to gleaning corn and haymaking.

Throughout this period, the drive for salvage collection was relentlessly pursued by all: paper and books, rags, car tyres, batteries, jam jars and, above all, aluminium and iron. The gathering in of iron left a permanent mark on historic Hampshire. Many of the county's older buildings were shorn of their iron railings in this process. Every town and village had its collection for Mission to Seamen, Aid to China Fund, Parcels for Prisoners-of-War, Red Cross, Sailors' War Libraries and many more. The Women's Institute at Botley even had a Working Party knitting gloves for men working on minesweepers!

Petrol was strictly rationed, putting the private car virtually off the road. This had a deleterious effect on attendance at church services in rural Hampshire, at a time when congregations were being asked to offer prayers for their serving men. At Exbury and East Boldre, both Ministers, while

And he must march full many a mile,
And fight through change and charge,
Ere he promotes his Corporal
And makes her Mrs. Sarge.

SALUTE THE SOLDIER

The soldier is giving up all he holds most dear. What can we do to show our gratitude? We can salute the soldier by saving.   SALUTE THE SOLDIER

Issued by the National Savings Committee

Winchester and District SALUTE THE SOLDIER WEEK
APRIL 29th—MAY 6th
Target - **£500,000**

The War Savings drive, 1944 (HC, 1/4/44)

chiding their flocks, appealed for a bigger attendance 'when we are distracted and tortured by war'.

In spite of everything, cheerfulness did manage to break through. The Government's 'Holidays at Home' schemes were popular and were devised in part to make sure that people did not travel far from their home patch, both for security reasons and also because, even for public transport, fuel was in short supply.

Fareham's 'Holidays at Home' programme from the summer of 1943 survives and shows that this event in wartime Britain was a great morale-booster as well as providing many more opportunities for fund-raising. At Wallington, the locals enjoyed a Grand Fête with a Punch and Judy show and no less than three beauty competitions for Bathing Belle, Best Coiffeur and Ladies Ankle. Operatic tenor Robert Easton was the guest star at a celebrity concert in the Methodist Hall, while at Bath Lane playing fields men wrestled, children ran egg-and-spoon races and ATS and WRNS gave athletic and graceful displays of gymnastics to general delight.

These were real compensations for the privations of war. Moreover, by 1943 there were many signs that the nature of the war was changing and the emphasis had shifted from defence to preparations for taking the war back to the enemy. Probably the most noticeable feature of this, so far as Hampshire was concerned, was the influx of American and Canadian troops, god-like creatures bearing gifts of nylon stockings, chewing gum and candy. The village of Chilbolton was typical of many communities in Hampshire that played host to American servicemen. The 17th Airborne Division of the American Army, the 'Thunder from Heaven', was welcomed by the villagers and the many friendships cemented then are flourishing to this day. Winchester, Southampton and Portsmouth also welcomed the Yanks in force. Apart from their obvious appeal to the girls – and teenage girls had the time of their lives – their natural friendliness gradually overcame the hostility of some of the older members of the community.

The transatlantic visitors joined an already strong community of servicemen from other Allied nations but their numbers and the level of their equipment were something new and contributed to a growing sense of confidence, not only in the ultimate outcome of the war but that the end was perhaps coming within sight: there was a general feeling that the country was biding its time and, as a Portsmouth man put it, 'a quiet confidence had asserted itself in the citizens and you got the impression that Germany had shot its bolt and that

An American jeep embarks (IWM)

it was only a matter of time before a second front was established in Europe'.

Preparing for the Second Front

In the south coast towns, preparations and contingency plans for all aspects of Operation OVERLORD were the responsibility of Hampshire's mayors, town clerks and dock and harbour authorities where their boroughs would be at the centre of troop movements associated with the invasion. The Office of the Regional Commissioner and his staff met the above Authorities on a regular basis. Naval and military authorities joined the briefings and this group worked in close liaison with the War Cabinet and later with Admiral Sir Bertram Ramsay, the Allied Chief Naval Expeditionary Officer, and Generals Eisenhower and Montgomery at Southwick House.

An important aspect of the 1943 meetings at Reading was the preparation of a route plan for the invasion force as it would pass through the county on its way to the embarkation beaches. A Gosport man working for the War Department was entrusted with this task:

"A heavily guarded office despatch rider bought information from HQ at Southwick House to our secret location in The Avenue, Fareham. I was informed of camp sites which were within a four-mile radius of the beaches. My job was to devise the best direct routes from the camps to the coasts. I had to send each map back to Southwick House for confirmation and timing."

Southwick House's role as the headquarters for D-Day planning is well known but other Hampshire houses were also requisitioned for administrative work to support the D-Day programme. At Hartley Wintney, Bramshill – now the National Police College – became the HQ of the British Red Cross movement, raising money for humanitarian purposes including food parcels to prisoners of war and the sick and wounded.

Bramshill's vast rooms and picturesque surroundings were enjoyed by neighbouring RAF men based at Odiham and Farnborough and the monthly Red Cross dances were a welcome diversion.

As the war progressed and the vulnerability of Portsmouth Dockyard to enemy raids increased, the staff of the Manager, Engineering Department, were evacuated to Cams Hall at Fareham, eighteenth-century home of the Delmé family. Later the Dockyard engineers would be joined by a large contingent of Royal Marine Commandos who used the nearby Fareham Creek for manoeuvres and found the extensive wooded estate of Cams Hall ideal concealment for their secret operations.

Meanwhile, attention was being given to other aspects of the logistical demands of OVERLORD. On 22nd February 1944, the War Cabinet met to determine the allocation of essential workers for the southern ports. Dock labourers were high on the priority list for both Portsmouth and Southampton. At Portsmouth Dockyard itself, the huge labour force was well under way with the pre-D-Day programme. Some repair work was still the priority but as the war progressed the experience gained in action brought urgent requirements for the installation of new devices in warships and auxiliary vessels. Principally, this

was radar. A Portsmouth man remembers:

"In May 1944, I worked for three days and three nights continuously – meal breaks apart – on ships called *Bulolo* and *Largs*, putting in what was reputed to be £1 million worth of radio and radar equipment so that they could be used as HQ ships for the invasion fleet. Personnel-carrying landing craft were modified to carry rocket launchers. As an electrical fitter apprentice, I was engaged in wiring up the rocket launchers as they were fired electrically."

Southampton Docks too were at the centre of events:

"Our commitments had expanded to the New Docks. This was for dealing with the huge American-built personnel landing craft. We had to use the King George V graving dock, workshop and the dry dock to float the LCTs from America which came as deck cargo on merchantmen and dropped on to the dock as sections which were bolted together........ an order was received to give up half of the working space in the workshop which was not at first questioned. The area was stocked full of steel rivets, nuts and bolts. Finally we were told to vacate the whole building. On asking, 'Who says so?', we were told, 'Mr Churchill says so.' Nobody argued but two Nissen huts were built for our use."

At both Southampton and Portsmouth the welders were in full swing, day and night. The sky was a blaze of purple light which lit up the surrounding area, ironic in the sense that the black-out prevailed everywhere else in both cities.

The back-up support and supply roles for the invasion forces fell largely on the Naval establishments of Gosport on the western flank of Portsmouth Harbour. For at least a year before D-Day all of these had been working at full pitch.

The Royal Naval Armament Depots at Frater, Bedenham and Priddy's Hard were the principal suppliers of armaments. Ammunition dumps were built up here and at the other embarkation hards at Exbury, Marchwood and Stone Point. The stores at the dumps were required to be in a state of readiness by May 1944. Records show the RNAD Gosport had, by 1st May 1944, produced 50,000 5-ins rockets for shore bombardment, of which 30,000 were allocated for the Landing Craft (Tanks) (LCTs) on D-Day itself. In the week after, all the support warships were re-armed, making a final total figure of 6,500 tons of ammunition to the bombarding ships. After the landings had ceased, the work of RNAD Gosport carried on throughout the summer. Worn guns had to be changed in the bombarding ships – H.M.S. *Roberts*, H.M.S. *Ramillies*, H.M.S. *Diadem*, H.M.S. *Ajax* were among these as well as a number of destroyers. Ammunition was also

PHOENIX caissons under construction (IWM)

supplied to the American fleet. The cruiser *Augusta* alone received 7,000 tons. Frater and Bedenham prepared a total of 2,560 mines for both the Navy and the RAF.

Priddy's Hard at this period was staffed mainly by women. They were first recruited at the outbreak of war and by 1942 they were more than half the total labour force of 3,000. Women were employed on a variety of jobs more usually done by men. In many cases, the work was heavy and dangerous. For D-Day, their primary work was on explosives, shells and hand grenades:

"I was on 2 lb shells. Every so often we had to go over them to make sure they were ready for despatch. I had a terrible experience once, you

Some indication of the dangers of working on the PHOENIXs is given by this photo (IWM)

the hours were long at Priddy's Hard and, as D-Day approached, 12-hour shifts were not uncommon. Comforts were few and smoking here was strictly forbidden because matches or any naked lights were not allowed in the magazine. Instead, many staff took snuff in off-duty moments in the yard or canteen.

Close by Priddy's Hard on the shores of Forton Creek is the Royal Clarence Victualling Yard, together with Royal William Victualling Yard at Plymouth, the country's largest Naval Supply Bases, both dating from the Georgian period. Clarence Yard did the lion's share of supplying the invasion forces with fresh and dried food, clothing, blankets and footwear. Staff at Royal Clarence Yard began the process of building up stores for D-Day in 1942, taking on reserve depots in and beyond Hampshire. Apart from the need for extra storage space, these scattered outposts were a precaution against the possible loss of stores and equipment due to heavy bombing in the Portsmouth Harbour area.

Extra storing boats were introduced and three 10,000-gallons-capacity water tankers provided fresh water for the fleet when it was anchored off Spithead in April 1944. The Clarence Yard bakery – the same one which baked the ship's biscuits for Queen Victoria's sailors – produced an estimated daily quota of 20,000 lbs of fresh bread in

had to make sure there were no detonators in them, because once you pulled the lever in them, they'd explode. I turned one up and I noticed there was a detonator. I showed the charge-hand and he threw it out. If I'd touched the detonator I would have been blown up. All the young men had been called up and they kept the old ones on. The foreman lost his job.

"The ammunition was put into the stores by the pier. We put on big overshoes and greatcoats in winter. We had to lift the crates of shells on to great big trolleys and push them down to the pier. From here, the ammunition was loaded on to the barges."

As for everyone else employed in the yards and factories at this time, addition to the 13,000 lbs supplied by private bakery businesses in Gosport and Fareham. From the moment of assembly at Spithead to departure in June 1944, weekly tonnages of fresh meat, potatoes and green vegetables went sailing out from the Yard to the waiting ships just outside Portsmouth Harbour.

As recalled by a former member of staff, the scene was both epic and surreal:

"In 1944, I was a Stores Assistant at Clarence Yard. On the run up to D-Day, we went out daily to Spithead in one of the Yard's Storing Boats. The ships were so tightly packed you could practically walk across to the Isle of Wight as if you were on dry land. We used to go alongside each boat and tap on the hull, calling out 'Any bread today?' etc. It seems hard to imagine but that's how it was as the ships assembled waiting for the 'off'."

At the mouth of the harbour, H.M.S. *Dolphin* within Fort Blockhouse would play an especially significant D-Day role. In the early planning stages for the invasion, it became obvious that a thorough survey of the beaches of Northern France would have to be undertaken. This highly secret work was done by men of the Combined Operations Unit well before D-Day using pre-war holiday photographs of the coast to help the men to get a flavour of the actual beach levels and the rise and fall of the tide.

Information gained from these undercover night-time exercises rendered the job of the Submarine Service smoother than it would have been had no preliminary survey work been done.

Further up Haslar Creek, the invasion fleet's mine-laying force lay in wait. The 13th and 14th MTB Flotillas were based at H.M.S. *Hornet* and, at the word of command, their task was to lay a total of 562 mines off the French coast to defend the Allies' Normandy beachheads.

Out on the fringes of the Borough of Gosport at Lee-on-the-Solent, 24-hour air cover for the seaborne troops was the responsibility of the air crew at H.M.S. *Daedalus*. RAF and USAF pilots flew 435 sorties on D-Day alone in Seafires, Spitfires and Mustangs.

Back in Gosport, the internationally famed yacht-building firm of Camper and Nicholson assumed an unaccustomed but vital role. Four types of boat for the invasion forces were constructed in the Gosport yard. The biggest of these were the LCAs (Landing Craft Assault) of double diagonal wood construction powered by two engines, whose propellers were contained in tunnels to prevent damage in grounding. Carrying 36 men, the craft were armour-plated and designed to be hoisted in davits and carried on the larger converted passenger ships. The flat parts of the sides and bottoms of these craft

were constructed on jigs by women workers in what was part of the Mumby's Mineral Water Factory in North Street.

A type of beaching craft called a Surf Boat was manufactured at Camper's. Some were motor-driven, others designed to be paddled or rowed ashore by the troops. Folding canoes and SLUG boats completed the quartet of D-Day craft produced at this Gosport yard. The canoes were designed for the Special Boat Service and were made in such a fashion as to enable them to pass through the 21-ins-diameter torpedo hatch of a submarine. The SLUG (Surf Landing Under Girder) boat was a small, shallow-draught vessel which carried the linking and mooring equipment as it passed back and forth under the floating units of the MULBERRY harbours.

In the autumn of 1943, recruitment began for the vast labour force necessary for the construction of the MULBERRY harbours. Many of the component parts of these were built and tested at various sites in Hampshire. The docks and coastline of Hampshire were the birthplace of a large number of the concrete caissons or harbour walls codenamed PHOENIX. A total of 14 of these were constructed at Stokes Bay, others at Portsmouth Dockyard and Southampton Docks, Hayling Island, Lepe, Marchwood and Stone Point. Apart from the complex technological aspect of the MULBERRY programme, one of the most difficult problems encountered was that of recruiting enough able-bodied men for the huge workforce which the programme would require. The Government solved the problem in part by importing numbers of Irish labourers:

"It was very hard work, we didn't have the know-how or the equipment they have today. But the work went on very smoothly in three eight-hour shifts – there were no strikes or discontent, everyone just got on with whatever they were doing. I think for most of the workers it was great fun. Being young and carefree, I enjoyed every minute of it."

The young Irishmen were to prove a bit of a handful, as a Gosport woman remembers from her family's experience in 1943:

"We had two young Irish fellows and a more elderly man from Lancashire. The Irish lads only lasted a few weeks. I think they were too lively for my mother but the older man stayed with us for about six months. He was a strong Communist and was always talking about the revolution that would come to this country after the war."

The Prime Minister made a number of site visits to see for himself the progress on the MULBERRY project. His reception was lively:

"Winston Churchill came to see us once. He was cheered and shouted at and abused from the port-holes, so no one knew who was doing the shouting. Said he was delighted with his reception because the men had plenty of spirit and freedom, just what the country was fighting to defend!"

As we have seen, MULBERRY workers were frequently billeted on local families by Local Government Officers who were entrusted with this work and with powers to compel the reluctant hosts. In most cases, compulsion was unnecessary as people were generally only too pleased to help. At MULBERRY sites, temporary canteens were set up, often by members of the WVS, to feed the men or they were taken by bus and coach to the nearest British Restaurant.

Work on the MULBERRY harbours was almost exclusively the preserve of strong young men, but there were exceptions. When General Eisenhower paid a visit to Southampton Docks he was surprised to be told that the driver of a Bedford truck carrying ballast to the site was a 72-year-old woman. She also held a pilot's licence.

Confidentiality and security surrounded the MULBERRY programme. Speculation among the workers was rife but confirmation of the nature of the units they were building remained a secret to the workers until after D-Day. The project proceeded with clockwork precision for over six months but accidents happened, some of them fatal. Three men died at Stokes Bay when one of the caissons slipped and jammed on its launch. Another man died at Southampton Docks when he missed his footing in the dark and fell into the dry dock.

Hampshire women play their part

One of the most striking features of the D-Day preparations is the extent to which women workers were involved in key positions. Whether in the Armed Forces, factories or the voluntary sector, women were central to the success of the OVERLORD operation, occupying posts which would have been unimaginable before 1939. We have already seen some remarkable examples but many more should be recorded. At the end of 1942, a dozen WRNS were appointed to H.M.S. *Dolphin* after their entry training and they worked in the Engineer's Workshop as mates to the Chief Engineer Room Artificers, as coppersmiths, welders and moulders. Among this group of women was Leading WRN Margaret Young, the Navy's only female blacksmith who, as one of her colleagues confirmed, 'swung a 14 lb hammer better than some men'. The *Dolphin* WRNS became famous and were featured in newspaper articles at the time. H.M.S. *Dolphin's*

Engineer Commander was proud of his female 'mates' and referred to them as his 'WRN-gineers'.

Hampshire's rural and woodland regions were worked by many branches of the Women's Land Army. Apart from the more traditional farming work, units of the Women's Timber Corps were based in the New Forest. Timber for various wartime uses was selected by the women and cut up, using steam engines to operate the saws. Ash was vitally important in the pre-D-Day period as it was a component part of the Spitfire's wings. The Women's Timber Corps were responsible for locating and cutting down the types of wood needed and they had to get permission from individual owners to enter every wooded area over an acre in size. Sometimes the owners were not co-operative and in these cases friendly persuasion was the order of the day.

In fact, if things got tough, cheerfulness invariably broke out. A sing-song raised the spirits and the Women's Land Army had a very jolly one:

"Are you lonesome tonight?
Is your brassière too tight?
Are your corsets all falling apart?
Does the size of your chest wear big holes in your vest?
Does you spare tyre reach up to your heart?
Are your stockings all laddered and your shoes wearing thin?

Do you hold up your bloomers with a big safety pin?
Are your false teeth all worn?
Do they drop when you yawn?
Then no wonder you're lonesome tonight!"

Hampshire's ports and surrounding villages accommodated a multitude of Service establishments and boatyards. Women played significant contributory roles in all of them. Samuel J. White's shipyard at East Cowes employed women. A trainee electrical welder remembers her experiences working on the destroyer, H.M.S. *Cavalier.*

"About 50 of us from Hampshire were put into digs with various families on the Island and when we wanted to get back to the mainland some weekends we had to get a letter from the bosses. Instead of being able to board the Isle of Wight ferry like any other person, we were escorted through parts of bombed Portsmouth by soldiers to our trains or buses. My home was at the back of what is now Southampton Airport, then H.M.S. *Raven* – Fleet Air Arm. I had to have a pass to get into my house. It was hush-hush all right."

RAF Titchfield was a balloon site with a large contingent of WAAFs. In the beginning there were a few problems to be sorted out:

"We were the first WAAF drivers in the camp and at the start definitely not welcome. We were put in an empty office with nothing to do except knit and after a while we complained as we were forgetting how to drive. Eventually, they were forced to use us. Some of the officers refused to be driven by women. I think they didn't have confidence in us to begin with."

Also at Titchfield, the Balloon Ops' girls had to be physically tough:

"It was a hard, lonely life out in all weathers. If it was stormy, the balloon often broke away and we worked with the duty driver to recover it. It was really a wretched job in winter."

Fortunately, back in the camp, a cosy atmosphere prevailed. There was the canteen run by the WVS in the village, opportunities to take part in sports, act in plays and attend dances with a variety of partners who were European and Commonwealth servicemen stationed in the area.

The WAAF drivers' working day started at 0800 hours, sometimes much earlier if a long run was the first job of the day. All drivers were responsible for their vehicles which included the Daily Inspection (DI) – check oil, water, batteries. There was night duty twice a week and all drivers had to do their own 500, 1,000 and 2,000 mile inspections. Despite the hard work, the women reckoned there were bonuses:

"It was never a boring job, always something different. We were in a nice part of the country, and the long runs were lovely."

Left: Eight land girls present a happy picture as they ride towards the photographer in this Fareham scene from the Second World War (IWM)

Right: Patriotic crowds line West Street during the war as a farmer and three land-girls pass by on a tractor drawing a 'Plough for Victory'. This was part of a big parade designed to uplift local spirits in hard times (IWM)

Right: Back-breaking work, but done with a smile. Land girls in the Second World War help the victory effort by picking tomatoes in Fareham (IWM)

Left: August 1944. First three WRNS cross to France (IWM)

The 13/18th Hussars move from Petworth to Gosport (IWM)

In and around Portsmouth, the camps were alive with WRNS. At Forts Southwick and Widley, pre-D-Day secretarial and cipher-coding units were established. These departments were housed in vast underground Chambers of Horror known to the staff as 'The Tunnel':

"It was an eerie experience to descend by endless flights of steps to the dark interior of the earth to find this huge organisation borne of the ingenuity of man, subtly lit by a brilliance vying with the sunshine above us, everything humming and buzzing with the urgency of the war effort. The climb up again at the end of a watch was the most trying part of all. Flight upon flight of steps stretched ahead and when we were tired and dirty, they seemed insurmountable. Two or three times on the way up, we would lean against the wall and pant, passed oftener than not by a grey-headed commander, taking the steps two at a time."

Once at the top, the WRNS were then driven to nearby Fareham where most of them were quartered. It was a rare opportunity to breathe in the smell of new-mown hay and the tang of the sea and catch glimpses of the harbour below by moonlight, soon to be filled with the D-Day fleets.

In the city itself, there were plenty of opportunities for star-gazing. A WRN stationed at H.M.S. *Excellent* remembers looking through a window onto the Parade Ground where a slightly embarrassed Lieutenant Laurence Olivier was parading a squad of Naval Cadets. Actors and performing artists were only too pleased to entertain the troops. The RN Three Arts Club was started in the Clock Tower in Castle Road, Southsea. Here, the concert pianist, Solomon, actor/author Noel Coward and Hollywood 'leading man' Robert Montgomery were among top-rank artistes performing for the servicemen and women of Portsmouth. Another Southsea venue was the elegant Frank Matcham-designed Kings Theatre, where regular Combined Services' Concerts were enjoyed, often played by the Royal Marines Orchestra under the baton of the immaculately handsome Captain F. Vivian Dunne. Further along the coast at Eastney, the Royal Naval Film Unit was busy making information films and documentaries of Service life at this

The 4th Battalion The Grenadier Guards with their Churchill Mk IVs between Titchfield and Park Gate (IWM)

period. This unit was responsible for the award-winning documentary, *Western Approaches*. A number of the Film Unit's staff had previously worked at Elstree Studios and their expertise ensured the accuracy of the permanent film record of these momentous times.

The dispensation of food, good cheer and homely comforts for the troops was the overall responsibility of NAAFI. The Institutes were to be found wherever concentrations of troops were stationed. A young NAAFI girl working at Fort Brockhurst, Gosport, remembers her service there:

"At one time we had the Commandos stationed there. They were doing their raids on the French coast and we all had to be confined to camp for three days for security reasons. Among the men I believe there were the Royal Engineers, the Warwickshires, Royal Pioneer Corps and lots of Canadians. All good crowds they were, too. We used to have really good ENSA concerts. Anne Shelton came to sing to us once, also George Formby."

As the count-down to D-Day approached, the Government canvassed the ordinary people of the country for their help in a life-saving scheme. Major blood transfusion services were set up in the larger Hampshire hospitals. In November 1943 the Royal Hampshire County Hospital at Winchester appealed for large numbers of donors to come forward. Evidently, the response was apathetic for the

Double parking at Paulsgrove during the build-up. Troops en route to Portsmouth (IWM)

Botley parish magazine reminded parishioners, 'that every available person in town, village, hamlet and factory should enrol to help this essential service'. The rector was disappointed to be told that out of his parish of 1,100 only 82 people had bothered to offer their blood.

The Royal Naval Hospital at Haslar fared better with its call in the spring of 1944. It may well have been that the people in the heavily populated Service towns of Gosport and Portsmouth were more immediately aware of the horrors of war and the necessity of a good response.

Tanks on the Doorstep

In the late spring of 1944, South Hampshire underwent a transformation. Into the lanes and highways poured a seemingly endless stream of tanks, lorries and armoured vehicles filled to overflowing with cheerful young servicemen from Britain, the Commonwealth and America. It was obvious that this huge invading party was intended for some colossal military expedition. This impression was reinforced by the mystery surrounding it, and people's suspicions were confirmed when at dusk clouds of thick, evil-smelling smoke floated over the streets now filled with troops and military hardware. This smoky camouflage was produced from large boiler-like canisters in the rear of some of the lorries and it was remarked that the smoke was at its most impenetrable on moonlit nights.

Possibly the most unusual aspect of the khaki invasion was the ignorance of both troops and populace as to the whys and wherefores of the operation. The troops, for example, had little or no idea where they were heading. All signposts had been taken down and officers were given only map reference numbers and times of movements when collecting their troops. Most of the transit camps were well sheltered in the woods and forests of Hampshire. In due course, other camps were set up in the environs of Southampton, Portsmouth and Gosport. Most precise timing had to be maintained as all troop movements were controlled by military police and any deviation from the pre-determined schedule would have resulted in chaos on the roads

because of the vast numbers of men and machinery which had to be kept moving. Any delay caused by traffic congestion would have had a disastrous effect on the final embarkation date.

But in spite of the hazards, the troops and their tanks arrived safely on the doorsteps:

"It was on Friday 30th May when we had the first troops in our road – it was only a small detachment but the previous week the police had been round telling all house-holders when troops came into the road we weren't to speak to them, give them tea or anything else, keep the children and dogs off the road. About 11 o' clock in the morning my wife was tying our dog to the clothes line when a voice said, 'Excuse me. Could I use your toilet?' She looked up and saw an Army Officer. She told him about the police and he replied, 'Some of my lads are on the look-out for the redcaps'. I got home at one to find four officers sitting in the garden, we also had troops in the drive. They all had tea while a friend kept watch. My wife also gave tea to the troops in the drive. They didn't get anything to eat till 6 o' clock. It was my son's birthday on 31st May, he wanted to give the men some cake, they said 'No'. One of the officers was a Yank, it was his son's birth-day the same day. He told me he knew he wouldn't see him again .... One of the men asked me where they were. I said, 'You must know'. He said none of them had any idea where they were. I told them, 'Gosport'. They still had no idea. I

then said, 'Portsmouth'. They all said together, 'This is it'."

There is no doubt that the khaki invasion was at first regarded with some degree of hostility. The famous British reserve was much in evidence. Initial reaction to the troops was that here was yet another inconvenience for exasperated citizens to put up with at a time when most of the creature comforts were in desperately short supply. It was yet another uncomfortable reminder of the ugliness of war brought right into the community. The ice-breakers were the children who began by begging for badges, sweets and chewing gum, all readily dispensed by the troops:

"Our son, then aged about eight, came home full of concern for the poor soldiers in their tanks having no dinner – couldn't we give them some? I said sarcastically, 'Let 'em all come to share our 4 ozs of meat!' The next thing I knew was my helpful son leading in two uniformed men who were a bit concerned at his insistence that I had personally invited them to dinner. What could I do but sit them down to our own meal apologising for the smallness of same and assuring them that we'd already eaten and, whilst they devoured that, hurriedly opened a jar of gooseberries I bottled that morning together with some custard made with powdered milk. I pride myself now I never turned a hair or showed the dismay I felt.

LCTs load at the Gosport Ferry Hard (IWM)

"My mother used to do a lot of washing for the waiting soldiers and once, when the whistle blew for the men to move off, she had the Padre's pyjamas on the line. She quickly grabbed them, rolled them up in a ball and ran down the road to the moving lorries. To the whistles and cheers of the troops shouting, 'Come on, Missus', she caught up with a lorry and flung the soggy pyjamas to the Padre to take to war.

"A soldier came into my kitchen and he stayed behind after the others had gone. He wanted to look 'just so' to go over there and I had to press his cap. He had a jet and silver rosary and he was saying his prayers.

"The strawberries were ripening and my mother picked all that were ready and gave them to us to take to the soldiers. After distributing the fruit my sister and I walked to Hardway to see the landing craft, all with their protective elephantine balloons floating overhead."

The coming of the Yanks brought elements of glamour, mystery and amazement at the variety and quality of their lifestyle on the roads. Their food supplies were legendary:

"My parents were hosts to a Captain and three Lieutenants of the US Army, 14th Port Establishment Unit. There were jeeps parked in our road near Southampton Docks and one of the officers sent a jeep to Christchurch to get a large piece of beef for my mother to cook Sunday lunch. It was the first time we'd had beef for years.

"Then along came the Americans, we treated them all the same. They stayed in every room while mum and I went down into the shelter. What a difference with all the things they had! They would say to us, 'Bring out your saucepans, dishes', etc., and they used to fill them with sugar, tea, coffee, tins of fruit, Spam, peanut butter. You couldn't believe your luck. We hadn't seen so much food since before the war. They were loaded!"

This was self-evident, particularly to the people of Hamble and Warsash. Many hundreds of US troops were holed up here and it became obvious that they were throwing excess food overboard. Local people were surprised to find whole hams, meats and tins of food brought in on the tide. Despite warnings by customs officers not to touch this luscious jetsam, some villagers shamelessly took the pick of the largesse.

British soldiers on the road were particularly aware of the differences. A soldier with the Green Howards was with his regiment in one of the sealed areas of the New Forest:

"I think our first impression of the Yanks was of the comparative luxury of their arrangements, particularly their washing facilities ... We were constantly amazed at what we considered to be their extravagant behaviour. I remember on one occasion watching a mechanic who had been servicing a tank transporter, his hands covered in black grease. He casually laid a jerry can of petrol on its side, opened the cap and washed his hands as the contents gushed out. We looked on open-mouthed."

The American Airforce arrived in Hampshire in both secret and spectacular fashion. At Christchurch towards the end of 1943 local people heard a great commotion along Mudeford Lane as giant earth-moving vehicles appeared, a sight never seen before. They moved to the southern end of the airfield and, pausing only to put the River Mude into a culvert, drove eastward, levelling all before them. The giant machines moved non-stop until they reached the Highcliffe-Lymington road. Residents watched in astonishment as the men proceeded to cover the bare earth with wire netting, apparently known as Sommerfeld tracking.

It was noticed that the men all had strange accents, hardly surprising when it was discovered that they were from the American 833 Airfield Construction Engineers. Soon the surrounding countryside was deafened by the roar of powerful engines as a fleet of American Thunderbolt fighter-bombers arrived to test out the spanking new runway, which was now nearly a mile in length.

In March 1944, large numbers of American Airforce men arrived at Christchurch Station and they were accommodated in temporary buildings adjacent to the elegant house of Bure Homage. Advance Landing Ground 416 was all ready and correct.

With Hampshire now saturated with troops and hardware, the 'top brass' were sometimes to be spotted visiting the sites and checking on the readiness and fitness of the men and their machines:

"Living in Cosham as we did then, we were very near Portsdown Hill and it was our own special playground for primrosing, bluebelling and blackberrying. We all had our special places which we kept secret from others. We considered the Hill ours. One day we saw a convoy of large and khaki-coloured cars. Our dog ran into the path of the cars and as the convoy stopped I saw a wonderful old gentleman looking at me who I recognised as General Smuts, the South African premier."

Winston Churchill seemed to be everywhere in the country. Often accompanied by General Montgomery, the Prime Minister visited factories, docks, special D-Day depots and the camp sites. On one occasion they both appeared at Sarisbury

LCTs waiting to set off. The nearer vessel carries one of the few Sherman tanks equipped with the British 17-pdr gun. (IWM)

Green, which, together with Brooklands Park, had been transformed into a vast transit camp for British and Commonwealth troops. Barbed wire surrounded this erstwhile cradle of Hampshire cricket and a Sarisbury man, then a schoolboy, remembers the efforts to keep villagers and soldiery apart:

"Despite orders barked out over the camp loudspeakers, patrolling sentries couldn't keep out inquisitive children and keep in determined soldiers. I saw a few French-Canadians use their tent mattresses to scale the wire in order to get at the likely lasses – children crawled under the marquee canvas late in the evening and we saw some fine shows, including Jessie Matthews and I think Gertrude Lawrence. The tunes of the day were 'Paper Doll' and 'Spring Will Be a Little Late This Year'. Rather prophetic, in view of the bad D-Day weather."

Popular songs, shows and concert parties were morale-building and much in demand:

"After leaving school, I had a job as an errand boy in an outfitters at North End, Portsmouth. Within the shop, the girls had formed a concert party and my pal and myself were roped in to join them. We used to give concerts to all the troops that were massing in the city. In fact, our shows were almost non-stop, for, as part of the audience – servicemen and women – were called away, another lot took their place. We used to call ourselves the HEPCATS and we rehearsed in the Mother Shipton Public House. One of the staff used to come round and take bets on the date of D-Day – it was the only time I remember winning a lottery. I was the only one in the shop to get it right."

At a time when no one knew what the future might bring, many romances blossomed between the troops and the local girls. A then 16-year-old Bournemouth girl remembered hers:

"I had a very sheltered upbringing. Bournemouth was very sedate in those days and rather posh! One Sunday morning I walked my dog past an American billet. This young American was all of nineteen, dark-eyed and curly-haired. It started with a shy smile and a remark about my dog. From then on we met by accident or design. The time flew for us, we walked, talked and shyly kissed. My parents knew nothing of this until one evening when I missed the last bus from Bournemouth Square. I rang him at his billet and he came round at once and drove me home in a jeep. Now I could introduce him to my parents, but as a friend of a friend. They took to this young American and – joy of joys – issued an invitation to tea for the following Sunday. We kissed goodbye behind a laurel bush and he drove down the hill out of sight. Later that night I woke to sounds of heavy vehicles moving and whistling and shouting. Running to my window I saw in the moonlight the troops were leaving. I ran out of the house in my dressing gown and down the hill frantically looking for him. Over the roar of the engines, voices were shouting, 'Goodbye, Honey, we'll be back'. Many of those young boys died on Omaha beach. I heard no more of him. I went back to my job, keeping my heartache to myself. I have been happily married for forty five years but each D-Day anniversary unlocks the memory and I shed a few tears for that bitter-sweet time."

As D-Day approached, the troops were moved close to their embarkation points and had by this time been issued with their special invasion money. Remaining coppers were thrown to delighted children waving them off as they boarded their landing craft but before that many shopkeepers benefited as troops bought up quantities of soap, toothpaste and brushes and other assorted toiletries. During their waiting time on the road, many men had found themselves severely short of cash and at one stage troops were to be seen knocking on doors on the Wickham road with army blankets for sale in exchange for beer money. Alas, at this period many pubs ran dry, although whether this was because of a huge increase in customers or a deliberate shortage from 'above' to prevent troops from drinking too freely can only be conjectured.

Down at the beaches the troops were in a state of readiness. At Fort Gilkicker, an ATS officer witnessed the loading up of vehicles at Stokes Bay. She wrote in her diary:

"The tanks have the full kit on board, even down to push-bikes and kettles. A Dakota is overhead, all striped up, the planes are not giving radio signals, everything points to battle ... landing craft up at the pier like whales, great jaws opening and swallowing the apparently infinitesimal beetles, which are in reality great monsters equipped with huge guns."

Finally, a little knowledge proved a useful thing. A Portsmouth-born soldier serving in the Guards Armoured Division Signals remembers his Division's departure from

Wounded arriving from Normandy
(IWM)

the Gosport Hards on D-Day plus 11:

"When our LST at last pulled out it
was dark and after a long day we
all slept. I was awakened at first
light by a shout of 'We are here',
only to see, when I looked out, the
War Memorial on Southsea Front.
We had sailed as far as Spithead."

All Quiet on the Streets

As dawn broke over the coastal
towns of South Hampshire, people
knew instinctively that something
truly momentous had happened.
The troops in their tanks, armoured
cars and wagons had vanished. An

Not all nurses worked in England: these are the first US nurses to land in Normandy (US Army)

all-pervasive air of unreality hung over the quiet streets. The early morning air of the 6th June was unseasonably cold and a grey mist intensified the strangeness of it all:

"The field opposite us was empty and the roads which had been packed with army vehicles were absolutely cleared. It was funny really, not a word had been said. All along the road was written in large chalk letters, 'thank you, Cowplain and thank you Waterlooville'.

"I went to work as usual in the

docks. It was empty and so quiet, except for the noise of the gulls missing all the food they had been getting and driven up the river by the bad weather in the Channel.

"The house where I lived in 1944 is very high and from a top window glimpses of the Solent can be seen. For more than a week at the beginning of June that piece of water was crammed with ships, as was the whole of the Solent. On the 6th June, the sea was empty and that to me was the most dramatic moment of all.

"The sight of the whole of Portsmouth Harbour, in fact all the water usually seen from Portsdown Hill, all the water was invisible, it was so thickly covered by ships, it was impossible to see any space between them. It is my most vivid memory, but nowhere have I seen a photograph of it. I suppose it was as much as anyone's life was worth to take it. A shame as far as history goes, not to have that record."

By mid-morning, the BBC had confirmed what most people already knew in their hearts. The invasion of France had begun.

Towards evening, it became the sombre duty of the nursing, medical and rescue services to tend to the steady flow of wounded or dying troops. All of the county's hospitals were involved. Ships carrying the wounded sailed up the Solent to Southampton where patients were disembarked and put onto hospital trains and taken to the front-line hospitals. Haslar at the mouth of

Portsmouth Harbour was one of these. All the wounded stayed for a few days' emergency treatment, after which they were moved further inland to make way for the next batch of casualties:

"My most poignant memory of that time was of the days immediately following D-Day. Hospital trains painted with huge red crosses would rumble slowly through Brockenhurst Station from Southampton travelling at no more than 15 or 20 miles an hour for obvious reasons."

"I was Liason Officer with the Assistant Red Cross Commandant. I was summoned to St James's Hospital, Portsmouth. As the convoys came on the first day, those that were landed on the beaches were back in hospital that evening, some terribly burnt, mostly Canadians. My job was to talk to them where possible, get their addresses of next of kin and write to them to say they were safely back in England and make light of their terrible injuries. Some were only boys and very shy. I would ask whether they had a sweetheart and whether they would like me to write to her."

New arrivals were covered in mud and grime with filthy clothes which had to be cut off them before medical treatment could begin. Each man was spoon-fed by a nurse. There were no drip-feeds in 1944. For two weeks after the invasion all leave was stopped, so off-duty nurses

at Haslar would climb the boundary wall of the hospital facing the Solent and look out for the loaded hospital ships in the knowledge that their life-saving skills were to be repeated yet again.

The most seriously ill servicemen never made it to the inland hospitals and many died at Haslar. A VAD at Haslar remembers one soldier suffering from shell-shock. It took several Sick Berth Attendants to get him on a trolley to the Operating Theatre where he died before anything could be done for him.

The Royal Victoria Hospital at Netley took the bulk of the wounded landed at Southampton Docks. The grandeur and enormous size of this military institution at first over-awed both patients and nurses:

"I will never forget when the first batch of wounded arrived. Casualities had 'T' for tourniquet and 'M' for morphine painted on their foreheads by the medics, so that we should know the first aid treatment they had already received. Fleets of ambulances brought them to the hospital. I took my first patient in and also had to report to one of the wards. I turned a corner and couldn't believe my eyes. The corridors of Netley were said to be the longest in England and there, standing four in a row, were all these wounded men. I was very upset to see them and could have hugged them all, instead I just ran, couldn't trust myself to do anything else."

Nothing of this colossal medical

The first German prisoners arrive at Southampton, 7th June 1944 (Southern Newspapers)

exercise could have been successfully undertaken without the dedicated work of the hundreds of doctors and nurses in the Hampshire hospitals. Many of the nurses were very young and inexperienced, certainly with no experience of the ugliness of death and mutilation caused by war. One of these was a Portsmouth girl who

joined the Red Cross at the age of 14. She remembers the lectures given by off-duty Army and Navy surgeons:

"Think hard, you may need to do this. You must be exact, or you will be out. Please understand this."

She did, gained her certificate and found herself on duty at D-Day receiving the first exhaustion cases from Normandy. She was just 16 years old.

In the second week of June the first of the flying bombs appeared over the south coast and at Haslar the wounded were quickly transferred to the eighteenth-century hospital's cellars. Medical staff were instructed to get out of bed at the Air Raid Warning, put on tin hats and get under their beds until the All Clear went. Many nurses, however, whose dormitories faced the sea, preferred to watch tin-hatted as the approaching flying bombs roared above the Solent on their fire-belching death mission.

The sick and wounded from Normandy were followed shortly by the arrival of the first contingents of German prisoners of war. Heavily guarded Nissen huts near the main buildings of Queen Alexandra Hospital, Cosham, harboured the first of the wounded Germans. On the western side of the harbour at Hardway, Gosport, able-bodied prisoners were landed 600-800 at a time and marched under close guard to a temporary holding camp near Forton Barracks. They were held for interrogation after de-lousing and hosing down. Curious onlookers were aware of the pungent odour emanating from these bedraggled creatures, the smell attributed to the ersatz material from which their uniforms were made.

Curiosity was the over-riding emotion experienced by the local people who watched from their front gardens:

"The prisoners were pretty exhausted, generally placid, not what you would associate with the master race. They had amongst them a ten-year-old Russian boy, perfectly kitted out in a German uniform."

"There was a firing practice on a range near Forton, which terrified the prisoners, they lost step, thought they were going to be shot. It caused some amusement."

A Gosport boy, proudly wearing his belt with metal badges collected from the Allied troops was watching a consignment of prisoners marching through Hardway:

"One of the prisoners saw my belt, stopped and pinned a swastika badge on me. A Military Policeman chased him back in the line. I still have that badge today."

The process of the embarkation of troops to the Normandy coast and the return of prisoners and wounded continued into the summer months. There was a general feeling, echoed in the Press, that the events of June 1944 had in a sense been a catalyst for change in many areas of our national life. As the Hampshire Telegraph put it:

"The great invasion on the coast of Normandy holds all our attention

and, reading earlier in the week a highly descriptive article on the sudden disappearance of the services from the laden streets, restaurants, theatres and cinemas, brought the reflection that this sort of thing is happening all over the country, and in our own County in particular. The stimulation of our local life in the last few months has been a truly remarkable feature and will bear fruit in the practical cementing of the bonds of real friendship between the peoples of the United States and Great Britain."

D-Day was undoubtedly the watershed in the progress of the war against Germany and it demanded huge sacrifices of our servicemen and women, best symbolised in a then six-year-old Gosport boy's remembered conversation with a departing soldier:

"One of them had a round face and dark curly hair. He asked me about school and what I had done that day.
'Will you be here tomorrow?', I asked.
'No, I'll be away by then', he replied.
'Down by the Bay?'
'No, further than that – to the war'.
'Will you come back and see us after the war?'
'No', he smiled. 'I won't be coming back'.
I often wonder if he did."

CHAPTER SIX

D-DAY REMEMBERED

Ann Bailey

This Chapter is devoted to the recollections of servicemen and women who took part in the D-Day operations in or from Hampshire. In deliberate contrast to the previous chapters we have allowed these accounts to speak for themselves, with the minimum of editorial intervention. The reminiscences are included in full, so that the reader can get a sense of the person and their reactions as well as of the events themselves. With one exception (that of Mrs Borthwick), the accounts were recorded specially for this book, largely from people who have retained some connection with Hampshire. This is by no means a typical or representative sample, therefore, although interesting similarities of experience appear in several accounts.

Above all, these accounts remind us that behind all the plans and the statistics of Operation OVERLORD, the actuality of the Liberation of Europe was experienced at the personal level, and it was the commitment and determination, humour and courage of innumerable men and women, both in the fighting services and outside, which made the operation possible and ensured its ultimate success. These are the stories of some of those men and women.

Mrs Pamela 'Bunny' Borthwick, WRNS

I had always sailed and when my call-up papers came for the ATS I said no way was I going to be an AT, so I made a great effort contacting all the admirals and people in Beaulieu. They wrote saying that I was a great girl on a boat and that I must undoubtedly go into the WRNS and drive boats. So I thought that my future was made. But oh dear no, it wasn't.

However, it did get me into the WRNS, where I spent a pretty miserable time, cooking and cleaning and becoming a maintenance girl, gun-mounting and then eventually a driver. They taught you to drive on three-ton lorries which was good, so I quite enjoyed my time driving for quite a few months.

Eventually I got myself into boats' crews where I then wore the coveted white lanyard round my coat and, of course, when you were on duty you wore bell-bottoms and a sailor's white shirt, the white with the square neck, and that was quite fun. Unfortunately, though, I was not driving any boat. I was a stoker and that was a terrible time. This awful old engine in the Liberty Boat, it was a petrol/paraffin engine and it would stall on paraffin. I then had to wind like mad, get all the paraffin out before I started it on petrol again. It nearly killed me. I must have been a stoker for about six or seven months.

Susan the coxswain and I became great friends and we always had our ears to the ground of course. We discovered that the landing craft base HQ at Portsmouth, which had come into being then because they were obviously considering a second front, the Normandy landing, was considering having a barge, to run their Commodore about in and to do various jobs. So we said, 'Let's go along and offer ourselves, nothing

The crew of the Commodore's barge: 'Bunny', Joan and Susan (private collection)

like a bit of cheek.' We did and were signed on.

Three girls ran the boat but they had to have a man as a motor mechanic who didn't exactly appreciate being with three girls. We had a succession of them, they all thought it was what they called a 'cushy job'. The third member of the crew was a rather glamorous 40-year-old who had never been in a boat before, other than to row round the Serpentine. She became the social success of the party and entertained all the admirals in conversation while we were running the boat.

As for our duties, to begin with we laid the pollywogs, small moorings, which would then give place to larger moorings for all the landing craft which would be moored around the Solent and hidden away in the creeks from one end of the Solent to the other. Eventually mooring lighters came along and dropped great big buoys. There was no other boat around, only navy, occasionally a warship, the place was deserted. We heard that boats were beginning to arrive. Indeed they did. The whole place started filling up. Our job then became taking around flag officers to look if the moorings were hidden away properly.

Men got terribly bored, moored in all the creeks and we found we were very popular. We went round with the 'Bish', the chaplain from

The King taking the salute at H.M.S. Vectis (Force J HQ, Cowes) 24th May 1944 (IWM)

the dockyard, and he had a whole lot of beautiful 'comforts', large tins of honey and clothes, from well-wishers in the colonies I suppose. Some of the men got very depressed, they obviously knew that the invasion was coming, and we managed on various occasions to cheer them up and perhaps write to people for them.

At Lepe they were building MULBERRY harbours, we didn't really know what they were, even though we were part of the job. It was so well-kept, the secret, you never talked. There were very odd things which would appear occasionally in the Solent. There was this enormous thing which looked like a vast cotton-reel, that of course was the fuel pipe-line, PLUTO, which was laid across the Channel to the landing beaches.

ML 529 leaving Portsmouth Harbour with King George VI on board, 24th May 1944 (IWM)

The next stage was practice landings. They did these at Hampstead Ledge on the Isle of Wight outside Newtown and you can still see the concrete runways, still a bit of one there and at Bracklesham Bay the other way. They were out for about four nights and I can remember it happening, very cold weather. We went to Hampstead Ledge and there was awful gloom, they'd been there all night under canvas. I think one, if not two men, had died of exposure. Even with heavy clothing it was bitter and when we arrived on the beach they were blue with cold. Next time we took huge thermoses of soup and, my goodness, we were popular. The men were still freezing so we pulled off a huge hessian fender and threw it around with them and they soon got warm. It was all very emotional. It was a unique job and we were extremely lucky to have it.

We didn't really have any drama, with one exception, when we landed at Cowes on the Squadron steps. There was a strong south-easterly blowing and our coxswain very sensibly had said to the officers, 'Sir, there's too much wind, I don't think we can go in alongside.' They said, 'Hah! Perfectly all right coxswain'. If you're a mere Wrens' boat's crew you do as you're told. So in we went alongside the Squadron steps and sure enough the seventh wave came along and it lifted us bodily, the whole barge, right up and there we were sitting on top of the Squadron steps. So then there was a frightful drama and all these officers, a good many of them, usually admirals and commodores, all getting their feet wet trying to push the boat off when the next wave came.

There were exciting times too. Battleships were arriving in the Solent and we had to take messages out. On one occasion we landed some officers on H.M.S. *Rodney* and were invited to lunch if we could put the barge on the boat boom. A boat boom sticks out of the side of a battleship and there's a rope ladder on the end. Climbing any boat boom is a test of a girl's strength of arm but a battleship's boom is quite a test for a man's strength, which of course we did not know. I was very

fit from being a dancing teacher and decided to lead the way. When I had climbed the ladder I found to my horror that the wire stay did not come to the end of the boom and it meant pulling yourself on to the boom by pure arm strength. By some extraordinary contortion I made it and offered helpful advice to Susan behind me.

When I looked up I saw that the ship was lined with sailors, the whole side, as word had gone around that there were Wrens climbing the boom. They cheered us and shouted, 'Well done'. We were delighted of course but on looking down saw Joan smiling sweetly up saying, 'Oh! Please come and fetch me!' Boats came from all directions.

That was dangerous but it was one of the things you just did. There was another dangerous episode at the beginning of June when George VI came to review the fleet. He arrived at Exbury and had to be escorted. We led, as you always lead, and royalty comes last. After reviewing boats in the area, he was to visit the other end of the Solent and boarded a Motor Launch to go faster. We waited off Cowes for his return as our Commodore was then to board the launch to talk to His Majesty.

On his return there was a wind blowing and an enormous wash. Poor me, the bowman, there was

'Bunny' Borthwick in 1993 (private collection)

nothing to hold on to on the matting-covered foredeck. I had to do my drill and swing the boathook to catch on to the Launch. We went over this frightful wave to come alongside and I bent my knees in the usual way. I could feel my feet leaving the deck and I came down, bang, each time and probably wobbled a good deal. To fall in front of the King would be a bit much but I finally gained my balance and thought I must just glance up at His Majesty. So I managed to turn my head the tiniest bit and look up and there was His Majesty doubled up with laughter, he thought it was the funniest thing he had ever seen, a lurching Wren. To add to it he apparently told our Commodore that he thought we would look better in skirts. It really was quite dangerous. Nobody thought about it, you didn't. There were no life-belts.

In a few days they were loading up in Portsmouth harbour, a very large loading area half way up the harbour. Big landing ships were there. The Americans were there too, it was probably an American ship we were watching. One occasion we took all these admirals up there and held on to a pontoon to watch the loading up for the impending invasion. We hung on and I was hanging on to the stern. They had obviously seen all they wanted to see and they said 'carry on coxswain, let's go'. But aft (Joan) was busy gaping at all the ships loading up and as the barge moved out there was one Wren hanging on to a boathook left behind. All these admirals were jumping up and down shouting, 'Hard astern coxswain'. So coxswain went hard astern and at least three of these high-ranking officers, admirals they probably were, jumped off on to the pontoon and pulled Joan out of the water. She stepped out on to the pontoon with complete composure and said, 'Oh, if only I had a camera, Sir, to remember this wonderful occasion.'

It was a frightfully sad drama when we knew D-Day was coming next day. The barge was faulty and had to be looked at on the Hamble. As we went out of the harbour they were already setting off; going out with the small landing craft. As we went about there was a chap on stern of the boat in front, a small LCT, doing semaphore to somebody. So I who could do semaphore too said, 'Good Luck'. He replied, 'Meet me at the Queen's Hotel in three days time when we're back.'

I went to Queen's but he never came. By this time many crumpled landing craft were returning. I'm afraid the worst may have happened to him. It was amazing to be there on the spot as it actually all happened. It seemed like years but it was really quite a short time.

Stan Gamble
Ex 1873176, LAC
Armourers Assistant,
121 Wing, 2nd TAF, RAF

We had moved from under canvas to winter at Westhampnet near Chichester from October to March/April 1943/44. We now moved to Holmsley South in the New Forest.

These were busy days as aircraft movements grew more noticeable but not many people realised just how close the second front was away from us. We were still able to enjoy trips into Christchurch and Bournemouth, shopping at places such as 'Bobby's', taking the odd drink at a pub if the landlord first had enough to supply his regulars. But it was rare that any service personnel were refused.

Shortly before it became known as D-Day I was having some dental treatment. I had only just sat down in the chair when I was told that it was all off, which pleased me very much, not realizing what lay ahead.

Almost at once we were told that there was a list of movement available setting out a complete split of personnel into two groups. We were to have to wait for the reason later. Fifty per cent of every branch of the airfield were then allocated their place on a vehicle. Mine was a three-ton Bedford carrying emergency rations, some 40 gallons of M. Transport fuel, the same amount of 100% aviation fuel, an eight-man ridge tent, 20 mm, .303 in., and other small arms ammunition, and a selection of assorted equipment plus our kit for the eight-man crew: myself as driver, the second driver-cum-Bren-gun roof man and the other six in the back with the gear. We later discovered that the reason for this was that each section had its own allocation of vehicles. If at any time one should be lost there would always be something about to get on with the job.

Within 24 hours we were on our way to Old Sarum. Tents were already available for us and we were complete, after a fuel top-up for the next stage. All transport was fitted with long exhaust and air-intake extensions but not connected up. There was also a supply of strips of Bostick and Sealastic. Now we knew the reason for some specialist training some six months before. We were then given a fort-night's pay in invasion money (funny francs). I lost mine that same night at cards.

We very soon moved down to Fareham. Most streets were jammed with various types of transport; where the hell had it all come from? We were parked to the north side of the main street. The residents were very kind in supplying us with water to make a brew or to have a hot wash. Our supply was cold only, delivered daily by bowser along with our grub. They very kindly allowed us to use their toilets. They, of course, were mainly elderly folk who must have been very apprehensive at seeing so many young lads, average age 20, probably not much older than their grandsons or sons. They must have wondered, as we did, how many would make it. Some of the language must have made the hair stand on end. The lads forgot we were only about a pavement distance from the homes and there was only a canvas hood

'Invasion money' is issued – and signed for! (IWM)

between them and eight blokes try-ing to sleep on top of all that gear which was most uncomfortable. Well, I suppose it was to be expected.

I am not sure how long we were in this state of readiness. It certainly seemed one hell of a long time to us. Our truck had a portable HMV gramophone on board with a mixture of Harry James, Vera Lynn, Bing Crosby, the Andrews sisters and jazz records. We probably emptied the local music shops of any they may have had. We spent many an hour sitting on the pavement in the main street of Fareham playing our music. We moan about kids today but I wonder what the good people of

Loading transport into an LST (IWM)

of convoys on the move and a lot of air movement, we had little idea of anything other than that which the general public were able to inform us of; there were no trannies in those days. In later years, of course, we realized that Caen was the hold-up.

Suddenly, late one evening, we were having a drink in the pub when an RAF despatch rider (who just happened to be an old school chum from my home town of Worthing) ran in and told us to return to our trucks at once. It was not long before the long and slow journey just down the road to Gosport began. I often wonder what the local folk must have thought when suddenly the roar of all those engines died away and silence reigned once more. Did they have the time to offer up a prayer that we had little enough time for because of nerves and concentration?

We arrived at Gosport Hard as dawn was breaking. The landing craft had just pulled in, back from yet another trip to France. The great doors opened, the ramp went down and a few guys started bringing out wheelbarrows full of helmets, boots and other equipment with a lot of blood on them. I started to feel a little sick wondering what the hell was in store. Reality was now being brought home with a bang.

Now more of those earlier months of training were being brought into use, such as the backing up of a

that town must have thought of us. They were very tolerant.

In the evenings we went to the pub on the corner from us and in pooling what English money we had we were able to buy a few drinks. They must have had some extra rations as I can't remember ever being refused and of course

we had a great deal of sing-songs.

Rumours had always been rife that we as a Mobile Wing would be on the move as soon as D-Day was under way but not so. We knew that an awful lot of activity was going on down the road at Portsmouth and Gosport. Then it started. Apart from vast amounts

268071

The first US aircraft to land in France after D-Day: a P38J Lightning of the 9th US Air Force. Note the proximity of the strip to the beaches (IWM)

lorry on to the landing vessel. It did not take long to get it all sorted out; ramp up, doors closed, the throb of the engine and that awful stench of diesel. We were given breakfast and then time was our own. I went down below decks and found me a bunk, put my head down and from sheer nerves and exhaustion slept until about 0600 hours on the morning of 15th June,

through a massive bombardment I was told.

We were given a good breakfast and then went on deck to see France for the first time; very bleak looking and I and many others not impressed. I, for my 19 years, felt that it might be my first and last visit. An NCO said, 'If you want your bloody dinner get those spuds peeled', nice guy. As we sat at the

Sherman tanks practise landing from LCTs in the Solent (IWM)

stern doing this with little pleasure we had not reckoned with seeing some bodies floating around.

When do we move? The Tannoy tells us we are due to disembark at about 1440 hours. Some time in the region of 1400 hours we are told to get to our vehicles and stand by. The engines of the vessel begin to throb. I suddenly feel quite sick again. We are heading for JUNO

beach. Suddenly we slow and very soon run aground. The doors open, the ramp goes down, we have already made our waterproof connections and our motors are running. The acid stench of ship's diesel plus our own exhaust fumes start to clear with the surge of air that quickly flows through from that vast open front. Time to go. The first three trucks roll out only to vanish from sight down a bloody great crater. I stop before the start of the ramp. The guys got out OK, wet of course. The order is given, up goes the ramp and the doors close. Later, as the ship pulls out, we see that the tide is turning and we will not be high and dry. Then comes the news that we will have to wait until about the same time the next day, the 16th.

Now we are safe off shore and moving a little further east, not much else to do but natter and play cards. Not me, I'm quite happy to kip again, who knows what tomorrow will hold? Soon we are at rest and before I hit the sack I take a quick look from the deck and about half a mile inland on the rise of high ground is Wing Commander 'Johnny' Johnson's Spitfire Squadron, Canadians. We learn later that his was the first squadron to fly from liberated French soil, being serviced by the RAF refuel and rearm Commando. Up until the night of 15th June they had flown in daily and out at night from Ford near Littlehampton in Sussex. That night they stayed, the first ever to my knowledge.

The next day we had breakfast, did odd jobs, peeled spuds (those unfortunate to be in the wrong place at the wrong time) and then followed the same procedures as the previous day. By the way, I seem to remember that the food

'Water-proofing' transport (IWM)

was quite good but don't ask me what it was.

We are on the run in and ground smoothly; doors open, ramp down and the fumes clear, engines running, we start our run ashore. Steady revs and a slow speed assure a non-eventful landing. We now go between the white tapes, making

sure we keep to the rules we have been given as the minefields either side have not been cleared. Some quarter of a mile inland after passing between the sand dunes, we come to a large clearing area where we disconnect the waterproofing and wait until the whole ship-load is with us. Whilst waiting we see an

Troops in camp in Hampshire, 'relaxing before the 'off' (ENHT)

impressive array of stores of many kinds and start to feel a little better now. We all start talking to each other more and feel a little less like zombies.

Now the convoy starts to roll. Soon we see the first small village and some of its residents and what the war is doing to this country. Oh dear God, but no time to think about such happenings. A large staff car is coming towards us along with others of different sizes. Someone waves and I say to my mate, 'I wonder who knows me over here?' My mate replies, 'Don't be so bloody silly,

that's Monty and he's waving you over to drive on the right hand side of the road.'

Very slowly we wend our way to our destination, one of the first advanced forward airstrips, a wheat field rolled and laid with metal track running from north to south, some four miles from Caen and about the same from the beachhead and probably the same from Bayeux.

Now it is almost dark and we are on the top end of the strip. On the western side we scrape a shallow hollow in the ground under a tree, put a tarpaulin over it, have a quick shielded fire, make a brew, open K rations, find some chocolate, find our blankets and, with rifles and Sten guns with us, roll the Bedford over our abode and drop into a short but restless sleep. Next morning we realize what the hell we have been sleeping under.

Up bright and early (not too sure about the bright)! We made porridge from a block out of the Compo rations and had a few hard biscuits and managed a brew-up using one of the slow-burning fire blocks. Now we know where the modern fire-lighters originated. Then we opened a tin of boiled sweets and some cigs, felt a little more human at last and then had a shave using left-over tea dregs to save the water we had left.

Soon we heard the noise of quite a number of planes which turned

out to be Dakotas. They came in from the north, turned sharply and very low just south of the strip and landed close on each other's tails. At the same time a convoy of ambulances arrived from Bayeux. As the C47's disembarked the other half of our airfield personnel, the poor devils whose war was already over, were very quickly loaded and flown out extremely smartish. As the dust clouds rose into the air we had our first taste of shelling from the Panzer tanks that moved in from wherever and out again after giving us something to make us take notice. I cannot recollect any real problem from that episode.

Now, as things settled down, our training once again paid off. RAF Regiment Bofors were established. We moved over to the eastern side of the strip, vehicles moved to their allocated positions, blister hangars with their camouflage grew at an amazing rate and we were operational in next to no time. Our ammunition dump was just across the road at the southern end of the strip, to our surprise, fully stocked. A group of us were sent out at once to start belting up 20 mm cannon shells with the various types of tracers etc., and assembling the rocket motors with the fins and saddles. Soon we had a plentiful supply.

Whilst this was taking place, the unmistakable sound of our Typhoons filled the air, flying low

Carentan landing ground, France, with a mixture of US P47D Thunderbolts and a Spitfire. Note the matting which was widely used to provide extemporised airstrips (IWM)

and wheeling round almost above us as they landed smartly in the inevitable dust clouds. The shelling started again. Soon they took the water bowsers out and sprayed before take-off and before landing. By lunch all was looking good and our mobile cook-house was working well and supplying us with a real hot meal. What a treat.

In the time between our work we dug two pits with a strip of earth left down the middle. This held the tent poles and our gear. The pits were long enough to hold eight blokes, four either side, two side by side and feet to feet. We dropped spare tarpaulins in and I can assure you we were cosy, comfortable and below ground level by some $2\frac{1}{2}$ ft.

A Hawker Typhoon Ib, as flown from Needs Ore Point ALG in support of the D-Day operations (IWM)

Our work went on without much to hinder us. We kept our aircraft flying all the time and like all other sections kept a high standard of efficiency. It was always sad when an aircraft failed to return, we were very close to our pilots. It was always good when one turned up out of the blue having evaded the enemy or helped out of a scrape by the French. Alas, others were not so fortunate, God rest their souls.

In the early days shelling and some bombing took place at varying intervals. One day they came in at the rate of about 300 an hour but we kept up our work. I often went out and helped the bomb disposal boys to dig out unexploded shells. We had a surprise when we found that a few which had been manufactured in some occupied country only had sawdust in them. Well done.

The rubbish left by the army lads (quite a mixture) in slit trenches, ditches and under hedgerows was slowly cleared away. We found some auxiliary fuel drop tanks left by the earlier tank liberators and by cutting off the 'Rhino' protection covers were able to get at the galvanized inner tank. By fitting a down-facing tap in the end and at the top we were able to fill it with water, place it over a small trench and light a fire under it. What a treat to be able to wash and shave in hot water and to do some laundering. This was a luxury that our comrades in the army would have welcomed.

We never heard that much of what was going on up front. We only got snippets from unreliable sources. We were called to a part of the strip one day where a Queen Mary trailer had been put in position and as many of the personnel gathered as possible. Then a captured German 'Storch' spotter plane slowly circled, not very high. It landed in the space of a bed sheet and out came Winston to thank us and give us a little pep talk. He went and we got on with our jobs as before.

A jeep engine receives its water-proofing (IWM)

Walter Earley
295 Field Company
Royal Engineers

We spent three years in the Middle East backing up the Eighth Army including Wavell's Offensive, then finally the siege of Tobruk and then the battle of Alamein and then we cruised across to Sicily. From there we were suddenly told we were going back to England and we knew very well by then that the reason we were going back was to take part in the second front, which had been heavily publicized.

When we were told we were coming home from Africa to take

Self-propelled guns are prepared before loading (IWM)

part in the second front the general feeling amongst the troops was, 'What the hell do they want us for? They've got all those millions of troops in the UK, why don't they use them?' We had mixed feelings, partly a kind of pride to think that we were good enough to be asked to spearhead the thing and mainly I think the feeling of disgust that we should have to go through it again after three years out in the Middle East and all the things that we'd been through, some a lot worse than I ever saw.

We knew what we were going back for and all the time we were in England training we knew exactly what was supposed to be going to happen. We were going to get on some ships and ride across and land on the beach which was going to be very hostile and full of Germans and we were going to be flung straight into it. This I think was very demoralizing, to know that all this was going to happen to you. It was different entirely to the attitude we had when we were out in Eygpt because there we went on from day to day doing the things that cropped up every day whatever they might have been and we didn't spend months agonizing about it and reading in all the newspapers about how terrible it was all going to be and that casualties would be at such and such a level. Nothing to induce you to go at all.

We got home, had leave after three years away and then were called back to Ely in Cambridgeshire, a most God-forsaken spot in the middle of the winter and freezing cold. We went on training exercises to put bridges over various rivers. Then we went to Inverary on Loch Fyne and did landing craft exercises. Suddenly the whole brigade of troops up there, of which we were the engineers, came down to Fawley in Hampshire and we stayed there from sometime in March until just before D-Day getting used to the equipment. A lot of it was American and we were issued with quite a lot of vehicles we'd never seen before, international half-track armoured cars and stuff like that which I found great fun to drive about in. And I had a motor cycle all to myself which was also very handy when it came to popping off out from the camp.

We practised water-proofing our vehicles so that they would be able to come ashore in water up to two or three feet deep. This was a job that everybody hated, having buckets of kind of putty and slapping it on all the parts of the vehicle that were likely to be affected by water without upsetting the running of the engine etc. We did a dummy exercise going over on landing craft to Studland Bay, entirely different craft from the type we finally went to France in. I was driving an international half-track, the last one on as it were, pointing towards the bows. Behind me was a Sherman tank and we all knew what we were supposed to do when the gate went down: we were to drive straight off. I was all switched on to do this, wearing my steel helmet in the approved fashion. When the gate dropped and the vessel hit the beach the tank behind me had failed to put any handbrake on and it came rolling forward and the tracks of the tank exactly fitted the steel bumpers on the back of this half-track so they climbed up the back of the half-track which lifted the front about four feet in the air and there we

Milk delivery for a Sherman crew (IWM)

were stuck and could not get off the landing craft. So eventually they backed the tank up and I came down with a crash and off we went.

We found out straight away that this waterproofing was not as simple as it appeared because we had to take the waterproofing off the vehicles as soon as they landed because the engines started to give all sorts of troubles if you left it on too long. I found that half the chaps, when they pulled the wires out of the ignition, stuck them back in the wrong holes, so half the vehicles wouldn't start again. I and some

48-hour rations are issued to the Green Howards (IWM)

place is now. It was then a big empty house with a lot of woodland around it and in these woods were loudspeakers slung through all the trees. In order to sort the vehicles out into shiploads, every crew on the truck was given the number of the ship they were to get on board. This meant that the whole of the unit was split up. There were only four or five trucks from my unit that were going on this one ship that we went on, in order presumably to make sure that if the ship went down they didn't lose a complete unit.

We all went to sleep around these trucks, with these Tannoys shouting out numbers all night, it seemed, until about four o'clock in the morning we all woke up instantly and said, 'That's our number'. It's amazing how you can listen to a number when you're sound asleep. We climbed on the truck and drove off in the early morning down the Hursley Road into Chandlers Ford. I can remember coming into the main road at Chandlers Ford in this convoy of trucks and all the men going to work were standing there. They knew darn well what we were doing and they were making quite a demonstration, 'Good luck lads' and so on, and we eventually drove down into Southampton down to what is now Mayflower Park but then was just a railway siding along the front of which they'd built ramps of concrete blocks to enable

other mechanics spent a happy hour sorting out the spark plugs and getting the engines to run. Nobody thought this was quite the right thing to do during an invasion. More lessons were learned.

We then went back to Fawley and eventually ended up on the road outside the oil refinery, the road down to Blackfield, and I found myself parked outside a house where the lady was devoted to bringing us out cups of tea all day and we sat there and thoroughly enjoyed ourselves, having the admiration of the locals etc., until we suddenly got shifted again out into the Forest somewhere near Brockenhurst on an empty piece of forest where we spent another 24 hours and then off to Hursley Park near Winchester where the IBM landing craft to come right up and drop their gates straight on to the level of the sea front. We spent ages sitting around in thousands of vehicles blocking that Western Esplanade completely. We had strict orders not to move, not to get off the vehicles etc. but somehow or other we found there was a little shop up one of the side streets there under the wall (it's not there any more, I looked the other day) and we were starving hungry. Amongst everything they'd forgotten to give us anything to eat. I went up to this shop and the old lady running it, I told her what the situation was and we bought a loaf of bread and she gave us half a pound of butter which must have been from under the counter and a pot of jam and we all sat round eating this illicit bread and jam and luckily nobody spotted us so we didn't get punished.

Eventually our turn came to go on board on one of these big US landing ships and these had upper and lower decks. The bottom deck was reserved for tanks and the upper deck for vehicles. Every one was packed in tightly and so there must have been about 40 trucks on the upper deck. We went off down almost opposite Hythe Pier in a queue, just like parking in a street really. The MULBERRY harbour was lying all down the side of the water there in Dibden Bay. We had no idea what it was for then but there

Walter Earley and comrades in France (private collection)

were massive great pieces of concrete which had been floated in after being manufactured somewhere else I suppose.

The weather was terrible, it rained and blew and we were all sitting around wondering what it was all going to be like and they suddenly announced it was off. So we all sat there. Once again the food situation was such that they had enough rations on board for one day but not for two days so we went rather hungry the next day except that they hastily produced food which was brought out to us. I was quite

surprised to find that this landing ship had its own bakery on board and the Americans were busy cooking bread. The first white bread we had seen for years. It was absolutely snowy white and I'm afraid it was also completely tasteless. But it was obviously the kind of bread Americans liked and this is what they cooked. There was also coffee on constant tap from various, I think they called them silexes, from around the ship. Tea was out. It was coffee or nothing.

We sat around and sat around and suddenly the following night we picked up anchor and off we went.

It was in the evening. It must have been six or seven o'clock I suppose. That would have been 5th June. Once we got out the other side of the Isle of Wight the ship started rolling unmercifully. It was extremely rough out there and the sky was full of great black clouds and the light was disappearing. I remember leaning on the rail of the upper deck of this ship and looking back at the Isle of Wight and wondering whether we would ever see it again. It got pitch dark and rained. The ship was rolling so badly that all the vehicles on the top deck had to be chained down tighter. We'd chained them down when we got on board but there was a danger they were going to fall over the side and we were crawling about under these trucks in the pitch dark on our hands and knees and finding the chains (we couldn't use any lights of course) and screwing the chains up tighter and we got soaked to the skin.

We eventually trundled off below to get any sleep there might be. None of us slept very much, pretty obviously, and when the morning came I went up on deck again and you could see a wild, wild sky all broken up with white caps, the wind blowing and great waves rolling along and a huge line of ships in front of us and another huge one behind and to either side.

Almost in front of us, one of these landing ships was towing a very large raft on which was a big mechanical crane or excavator with a long crane-like jib on it and the thing was sticking up in the air 40 or 50 feet I should think and it was rolling so badly that the raft was taken up at terrific angles and eventually the whole darn thing went completely upside down and everybody went merrily along towing the raft behind but I often wonder whether the thing was chained down still hanging on underneath or whether it simply fell straight to the bottom. The sea was actually quite full of debris, small landing craft, boats and bits and pieces of all descriptions were floating about in the water as we sailed along.

Our time of landing was supposed to be 10 a.m. so obviously a lot of people had gone in front of us because the first ships I think landed at 6 o'clock. We were due to land on Gold Beach which was the 50th Division beach. We were brigade engineers to that outfit.

Well, when the time came, we came up to the beach and there was no sign of any enemy activity in the air at all. We never saw a single aircraft at all. There was just an awful lot of stuff flying around but none of it seemed to be very much aimed at us. The shore was a confusion of spray from the waves. It looked like a foggy sort of beach where you could not see any detail at all as you approached it.

The landing ship came up to shore and naturally we were all up on the top deck looking to see what was going to happen. The waves that were rolling in were quite high and the ship seemed to us to stop quite early on. It didn't seem to get in nearly as far as it might have done and, as it turned out, as it ought to have done. So we dropped anchors right parallel with another American landing-ship and down went the gates, off went the first Shermans. They were already over their tracks when they hit water and every one of them, when they came down off the landing craft and got on to the sand, they opened up their throttles with a roar and the tank dug itself a little bit of a hole before it started off. So they were getting deeper and deeper and the tide was coming in rapidly as well, so that by the time all the tanks had gone they were up to their turret level in water.

We thought [the ship] is going to move in now, because no trucks are going to get off in this stuff, but instead of that, the ship didn't move in, it never moved in. We expected it to go in another 150 yards or so and drop the gate again. Not so. We were absolutely astonished when the first trucks went off, how deep they were in the water. One, I remember, was a breakdown recovery

Right: A P47D Thunderbolt of the 367th Squadron USAAF crash-landed on a forward airfield in France. Ground crewmen spray the aircraft with foam and help to extract the injured pilot.

Left: Hawker Tempest V of 3 Squadron RAF. The two aircraft in flight are on their way to patrol the D-Day beach-head.

crane, a big American thing and the water was up in the truck body already when it came off and it went about 50 yards and conked out. You could see the tide rising along this truck. Other vehicles were still coming off afterwards and some were managing to stagger away, others were just disappearing and getting washed away. There was a tremendous side current as well. This breakdown truck, in no time at all it seemed, only the jib of the truck was showing above the water and the crew of it were standing on the jib looking rather helpless until they just got washed off it and they put a dinghy out from the ship with American sailors in it going round pulling chaps who were swimming in the water on to the dinghy and bringing them back to the ship.

So we thought this was crazy, they were surely never going to carry on, but we didn't move and eventually I saw a 15-hundred-weight Bedford truck drive off the gate and completely disappear. I think they then realized that it was pointless in putting all these trucks out because they were none of them going to get anywhere. I've no idea why we didn't move, no idea who had to obey orders. Because we were broken up in our unit, we only had four or five of our own people on board, we had no chain of command. We just had to stand there and let things happen.

After what seemed like hours, the ship backed off and anchored off-shore in deeper water with us still fuming away on board it. We stayed there until the tide started to turn and then we saw that the other American landing ship right next to us hadn't moved either. It couldn't move because it was sitting completely on top of a Sherman tank. The bows of this landing ship had somehow or other managed to get right over this Sherman tank and was sitting on its turret. Whether there were any crew inside it or not I wouldn't like to say, but they were there through the tide.

We then stayed there off-shore all that night, while all the rest of our outfit, of course, were already well on shore. You can't imagine how we felt about it. I think I much preferred to be in on the landing than out in this ship.

Anyway, as soon as it got light again the next morning, they brought a big raft up, what they called a Rhino ferry, a huge thing composed of steel tanks bolted together. On the back of this raft were two huge outboard motors with American seamen on each one, opening and closing the throttles and steering the thing. These two big outboard motors just pushed this huge great raft along and brought it up to the ship and we all drove off neatly enough on to this raft and they shoved it on shore and

we drove off the raft down some ramps on to the beach.

The beach was littered with tanks and vehicles of all descriptions, there were literally hundreds of vehicles abandoned. They'd been under the tide and the tide was on its way out for the second time when we came ashore. I was driving a big break-down vehicle, an English make called a Carrier and I was all on my own in this truck and I wanted to make darn sure that I didn't join this crowd of people who were stuck in holes. The beach wasn't a good beach at all, there were lots of soft clayey patches into which a lot of these vehicles had driven and got stuck. They couldn't see what it was like when they were driving ashore in water, of course. I had to dodge all these holes and drive around various broken down bits and pieces, tanks and all sorts until I got to where the coastal road or promenade ran along the beach and I gave a last heave and up over the top I got on to the road itself. There was a road pointing straight ahead and I thought that must be the one to take. There was nobody there to say anything at all, it was absolute chaos as far as I could see and there was just a little board saying 'Beware snipers' which I thought was very handy.

I drove up this road to Bayeux because I'd seen maps and I knew more or less where we were. We landed at a place called Le Hamel on the right flank of the 50th Division which is very near to Arromanches where the MULBERRY harbour was eventually installed.

After I'd driven the truck for about a quarter of a mile I found I couldn't change gear on it any longer because there was salt water in the gearbox. I pulled in off the road into an entrance of a château, a big wide entrance in which there was an ash tree growing in full leaf. Somebody had shot nearly all the branches off it and I found out why when I stepped out of the truck. I stepped straight out on to a dead German who had been manning a machine-gun near a hole at the entrance to this château pointing straight down the road. Obviously a tank coming up the road had just opened up with their machine-gun which would account for all the branches coming down and this poor chap was buried underneath them. So that was my first touch of French soil with a dead German between me and it.

I drained the gearbox off. I was lucky to be in a breakdown truck, I had everything on board I could possibly want.....and off I went. I eventually found my unit sign and got welcomed with open arms. The mechanics in the company spent the next four or five days going down to the beach, finding our own vehicles. They were being hauled out by the Royal Electrical Mechanical Engineers I suppose, and stacked along in ranks in the fields. There were acres and acres of lines of vehicles of all descriptions and you just drove along until you saw one of your own and hooked a rope on it and towed it up to where we were camped and we spent the next four or five days with practically no sleep at all trying to get all these vehicles running again after they'd been under the sea for 24 hours.

We got them all going. The old man's jeep was the one I started on, because that was the most important vehicle of course. It was quite an exercise in ingenuity to get all that lot running again. God knows what would have happened if we had had an opposed landing, I don't think we'd have stood a dog's chance. But as it was, our landing, our particular landing was a bit of a fiasco and that's really the story of D-Day as far as I was concerned

Commander John Goulder RN, Petty Officer in H.M.S. Goathland, a Hunt class destroyer

Force S sailed from Portsmouth and the Solent on 5th June 1944. The leading group, S3, led by *Goathland*, was responsible for the direction, control and support of four Landing Ships (Infantry) and their numerous LCAs carrying the 8th British Infantry Brigade, five Landing Craft (Infantry) carrying troops of the same Brigade, as well as 66 LCT, carrying tanks and support vehicles of the 27th Armoured Brigade.

For close support during the assault there were also 48 Landing Craft (Support) of various types and sizes, carrying a variety of weapons from 4.7-inch guns to 'Hedgehog' ahead-throwing weapons normally used in anti-submarine warfare, but now for clearing beaches of oilslicks and mines.

On the morning of 6th June *Goathland* followed her LCTs of the first wave in, being forced to hold off 3,000 yards from the beach as the water shoaled to four fathoms. She remained offshore throughout the day and the next, controlling movement between the Transports and the beaches.

When the Force formed up in the Solent in the late afternoon/evening of 5th June, the taking up of formation by all the various craft was a wonderful sight. I believe we were all confident that this operation would be a success, a reward for the many hours of training we had undertaken, often in poor weather in the Moray Firth in Scotland, and that, moreover, it would also bring to an end the war in France. At the same time, we expected to receive a

H.M.S. Goathland (Cmdr J. Goulder RN)

'warm' reception once we neared the beachhead. We did not think it very likely that we would be attacked on the way across.

As we left the Solent the ship's company was closed up in defence watches (half the armament was manned). Religious services were held for the various denominations on board. A Church of England service was held in the wardroom by a Commando chaplain, Maurice Woods, who later became the Bishop of Norwich. I remember thinking that there were many faces present not normally seen at church services and attendance was not compulsory on that occasion.

Once clear of the Solent and formed up for the crossing, the ship's company went to 'Action Stations', ie. the first degree of readiness. My action station was in the Transmitting Station (Gunnery Control Centre) and I saw nothing more of the Force until the landings started the next day.

Our ship's company consisted of about 177 officers and men and we had on board a total of about 284. The additional numbers were Forces staff and liaison personnel. Shortly after we had checked that the armament was ready for action, someone knocked on the door to our Control Centre. When we opened up a Commando Officer and his Sergeant asked if they could sit with us until arrival at the other side. I thought it was a good idea since it would provide a change of conversation. Both were well-armed with side arms and the usual commando knife. We talked the night through about all sorts of subjects, avoiding politics and religion which is the naval custom. Never once did they say who they were, what they had done or what they were about to do. In the early morning, as we approched the beachhead, they left us as quietly and politely as they had arrived. I have often wondered how they fared and if they obtained their objective.

We had been informed of our progress over the ship's communication system and as we approached the landing zone were expecting to hear from the 'reception committee'. Much to our surprise, little happened.

Unlesss directly attacked, the ship was not to open fire since gunfire vibrations were likely to upset the many wireless communication sets that we carried for Force communications. Thus when the landings started, and as there was no off-shore opposition, we were able to come out on deck to witness the craft go inshore. I well remember the waves of Landing Craft (Infantry) passing close by, the faces and actions of confident soldiers clearly visible as they waved and patted their automatic weapons. At about this time the heavy ships were bombarding over our heads and the Landing Ships (Rocket) were going in four abreast and swinging from side to side firing a massive blanket of rockets. It was the most devastating sight I have ever seen.

We had what we called 'action messing breakfast' – meat, sandwiches and tea – which was well received, as we had had only cocoa to drink since the evening before.

By this time a coastal battery of large calibre guns seemed to have found the range of our beachhead and was firing occasionally in our direction. From the splashes, some of which were quite close by, they seemed to be of about 11-inch calibre. I do not remember any spectacular happening during the day. Equipment continued to proceed ashore. It was an impressive scene. We were greatly reassured by the Allied aircraft which gave us overhead cover.

In the early evening we saw a vast 'air armada' approaching the beach. As the droning of the aircraft intensified, we could see the gliders in tow. There seemed to be hundreds. I believe they were the backup for the Para force that had landed early the same day. We stood spellbound on deck as these great machines wheeled overhead on the run to their dropping zone, releasing their gliders which majestically and silently swooped down. Several of the towing bombers were hit and one severely on fire astern was losing

Goathland approaching her fuelling berth in Milford Haven (Cmdr J. Goulder RN)

height as he flew out to seawards right in our direction. We were in a quandary whether to run to the bows or the stern but the pilot saved us the problem as he managed to avoid all the vessels beneath him. I recall we said at the time that if there were special seats in Valhalla then he and his crew were due for them.

Nothing much of note occurred during the next two days, not that I recollect anyway. In the morning of D-Day plus 3, at about 0400 hours, we were told to prepare to land any men that could be spared to assist in general work on the beach and to unload stores for the front. Several men were sent to the galley, where sandwiches were prepared, and packed the lunch of those who

were going to land. Being keen to see what was going on I volunteered to land and, with some of the ship's officers and about 30 of the ship's company, embarked in a landing craft about 0800 hours, proceeding round various ships and craft to collect any available labour.

The passage inshore was uneventful until we approached the beach. Just after the ramp was lowered we came to a grinding halt. We learned later that we had hit a submerged DD tank which had been lost on D-Day. The tide was ebbing and we rapidly began to turn over. We disembarked into about four or five feet of water, boxes of food held high above the head.

I suppose it was some 50 yards to

the shore line. I remember Able Seaman 'Shorty Halcrow', who was barely five foot two in stature, disappearing below the surface tin hat and all. He had walked into a hole. I and another raised him to the surface and I recall the immense grin he had on his face as we did so.

Once ashore, we emptied our boots of water and set about unloading some craft high up on the beach; others were allotted the task of clearing the beach of obstacles such as huge tree trunks which took 30 men to lift. We gradually dried out during the morning and had a break for lunch of sandwiches and lime juice. As the tide came in so did several landing craft with stores. Much of this material was whisked away by DUKWs to the Forces inland. Some went by truck.

The craft that had to be unloaded on a rising tide also had to be kept at right angles to the shore line. To stop them broaching to, we were back in the water up to our waists holding them against the sea.

I went ashore on three consecutive days. The second day we had German prisoners to assist us. Most that I had were the more middle-aged men who co-operated well and seemed happier where they were than where they had been. A few, mostly the younger element, refused to work and were left in the charge of the King's Own Regiment. The Senior NCO marched this gang

up and down the beach all day until the Landing Craft arrived to take all to a POW camp. On my third day I was given the job of clearing some damaged landing craft of explosives and ammunition and sending these to a dump inshore.

My bright idea was to give the 20 mm ammunition to the military who had several light anti-aircraft batteries near at hand. But to no avail as the naval ammunition was not self-destructive. We manhandled the various boxes to the road at the back of the sand dunes and to a truck that we acquired.

Some of the landing craft had a few of their crew in them: those who had been killed in the landing. The 'specialist team' arrived to effect the removal. I was moved by the proper feeling these men showed to the corpses they removed for burial. It was as if, with each, they were keenly aware they were dealing with some mother's son.

Some days later a great change in the weather brought a storm which wrought havoc to the MULBERRY Harbours and small craft.

Shortly after this, H.M.S. *Goathland* was to patrol by night and return to the anchorage by day. On one patrol we rescued from the sea a German airman whose aircraft had been shot down by a night fighter. His name was Helmut Kraft. I have now made contact with Helmut who has retired and lives in Bochum.

After many night patrols H.M.S. *Goathland* was struck by a mine off Le Havre in the early morning. Our good fortune prevailed – we had some injured but no-one was killed. We were towed back to the beachhead and then to Portsmouth where the ship's company was dispersed to its Port Division.

Bert Page
52nd Heavy Regiment, (Bedfordshire Yeomanry) Royal Artillery

On returning from Iceland during 1942 with the 536 Coastal Battery I was posted to a gun battery at Lepe Point near Calshot. During the latter part of 1942 a notice was put on the order board asking for volunteers to make up a heavy regiment of field artillery. This regiment would be taking part in the invasion of Europe when the time came, although this wasn't stated.

Along with about six other lads, I volunteered. We were to report to Fleetwood, Lancs. Arriving there we were placed in various billets, myself in a school. It took several days for the numbers required to arrive.

We found out that the regiment to be formed would be the 52nd Heavy Regiment, Royal Artillery. It would consist of four four-gun 7.2

Howitzer Batteries with a Regimental Headquarters. This Regiment had previously been with the BEF in France in 1940 but was disbanded after Dunkirk. The full title would be the 52nd Heavy Regiment (Bedfordshire Yeomanry) RA. The four batteries were numbered 417th, 418th, 419th and 420th and were to be called Heavy Batteries.

Everyone was given an aptitude test to find out his best abilities. I was put into the Signal Section and had to learn Morse [code] and the use of radios. I also had to drive, which created much interest amongst many of the lads who none of us had ever been behind the wheel of a vehicle previously. But it wasn't long before things began to take shape.

The gun crews had all fitted into various jobs. We signallers had intensive training, i.e. cable laying, manning field telephone exchanges, learning wireless procedure, linking up batteries in series, training in use of generators to charge batteries, and, as I said previously, learning to drive.

Eventually, after months of training, I was detailed as a wireless operator and passed my driving test, which gave me the title of driver operator and entitled me to wear crossed flags above a driving wheel.

On completion of all our training the Battery which was 418th moved to Orwell Park near Ipswich in Suffolk, about July 1943. Here we

A tank crewman breaks the ice with a flower (IWM)

were equipped with more modern equipment and the training intensified. We went to Otterburn for live shooting, during some awful weather. This place was on the borders of England and Scotland and never seemed to stop raining. There was also live shooting at Hunstanton, which was a disaster. Someone gave the wrong range to the guns which resulted in a farm house being badly damaged, but fortunately no casualties.

Then around March 1944 we moved to Salisbury Plain for a long series of practice shoots and much swatting up on wireless procedure. This was to prove very important when we did land in France.

The early weeks of May 1944 we moved to Southampton. Our tents etc. were on Southampton Common but all our vehicles were in the streets, along with the guns. The area was called Bassett and the streets were all named after flowers. Our particular one was called Iris Road. The residents were very good

Calm before the storm: in camp before embarkation (IWM)

everyone descended upon that establishment like a pack of wolves.

We had learnt to take some sort of drinking vessel with us as most pubs were without glasses. We took jam jars which was quite a laugh but at least we got a drink. The time arrived for us to leave Southampton and I promised Joan I would write to her, whatever the difficulties. By this time I had fallen in love with her.

Our move took place late May 1944 to Stakes Wood just outside Portsmouth. This was like a detention centre. Everyone was virtually a prisoner. No letters, no contact with any civilians, although this did happen when we had to leave the camp to service our vehicles, which were outside the camp. One chap who lived near Stakes Wood did go home without anyone's knowledge, except his mates. It was a risky thing to do as we could have been moved at any time.

June 6th came with the news that the invasion had taken place. We were rather disappointed not to have taken part in the initial landings but this was understandable as our guns were so big we assumed a secure landing would have to be made before risking our equipment. Nevertheless there was great excitement when on the evening of D-Day we were ordered to our vehicles with all our equipment to prepare to move off. This was what we had trained so hard for, for so long.

to us and despite the upheaval treated us wonderfully well.

It wasn't long before many of us, to use an old army term, had 'our feet under the table'. I got very friendly with a lovely family called Osman. Their youngest daughter Barbara, who was about seven or eight, used to talk to me a lot and was instrumental in getting me into the family house. They were a large household, consisting of Mother, Father and daughters Joan, Joyce, Brenda, Barbara and sons Bert and Gordon.

As time went by I was attracted to Joan more and more. We, that is the family, had some nice evenings indoors playing darts, skittles and cards and, occasionally, 'hunting' for some beer. This was quite an enjoyable venture. When word got round that some pubs had a delivery of beer,

We made our way to Gosport which, for such a short journey, took many hours. We did stop at the naval base H.M.S. *Sultan* all day on D-Day plus 1. We even played cricket with the ratings of the establishment. This was a good distraction and took our minds off the hazardous job that lay ahead of us. The evening of D-Day plus 1 saw the battery move to Gosport where the ferries ply between Portsmouth and Gosport. This was very nostalgic for me as it was so close to my home. We were there for some hours and spent much of the time drinking tea and smoking around the Dive Café. This was a well-known place for local bus drivers and did a roaring trade. We had no English money but all the people that used the café were very generous with gifts of cigarettes and endless cups of tea.

Eventually we loaded all our vehicles and equipment on to LCTs. This took several hours before we moved out to take up positions in the Solent. This was on D-Day plus 2, my birthday. An American patrol boat ushered all the convoy into its proper positions with loud music blaring out. The one tune they kept playing was a piece called 'La Composita', so whenever I hear that being played it brings back memories.

Eventually we set sail late at night with, it seemed, hundreds of landing craft of all types. Things were

Bert Page and his gun crew (private collection)

fine until we left the shelter of the Solent. Then the craft we were on, and I guess the others were the same, began to pitch and roll. The majority of us were sick for all the trip. Those who weren't sick did very well with all the extra rations that came their way. I suppose with not being very good sailors and the thought of facing battle didn't help our stomachs.

When dawn broke on D-Day plus 3 the coast of France was very close and the sound of shell fire was very loud. Also the naval craft that were laying off shore were firing their guns continually. Some of these were huge and the noise was deafening and didn't do our morale much good. Although thinking of the enemy at the receiving end bucked us up.

We eventually were told to start the engines of our vehicles and warned once we were in the water to keep the motor going at all costs. The ramp was lowered and away we went. The water wasn't too high so getting ashore didn't prove so difficult. Once we hit the beach there was much gesticulating by the beach groups telling us where to drive.

The first thing to be done was to de-waterproof all vehicles. This was done by sections of Royal Electrical Mechanical Engineers. Our trucks, lorries and all driven vehicles had been waterproofed so that they could be driven in the sea prior to sailing. Now all this had to come off and it didn't take the REME long to get them all ready for the road. This really was a work of art. The beach we landed on was GOLD, at Asnelles.

Once all this work was carried out the Battery moved inland and took up position for our very first action. This was quite an experience as all our work previously was practice but this was the real thing and all our training was now put to the test.

The beachhead by this time was still precarious and the thousands of troops crammed into it was colossal. The noise of artillery was incessant, as was mortar fire.

I was sent on my first op and was up with the infantry. This was really scarey, but I soon got used to it. It was a very difficult time for everyone with rations being scarce and not very appetising. Everything came in boxes and was called compo rations. The thing we longed for most of all was a decent cup of tea and some white bread. All we had was hard tack biscuits. These were not very appealing but a lot of the lads supplemented their diet with whatever was around. A good number of farmers had deserted their farms and the troops helped themselves to what was left. Milk was plentiful as the cows wanted milking and there were plenty of country lads in most units who knew how to milk. Some units 'adopted' the poultry for the eggs. Those farmers who were left bartered cheese and butter for cigarettes and chocolate. Unfortunately the cattle casualties were enormous and there were thousands of cows etc. lying in the fields, legs in the air and bloated. The stench from these was disgusting, especially when a shell or mortar landed close by and punctured the carcase.

It was a very unpleasant time for all the fighting troops, with no decent washing facilities and wearing the same clothes continually. But most made do and managed to keep reasonably clean. Diet was another big problem, with the lack of fresh vegetables and fruit. Skin problems were pretty rife. To compensate for the lack of these vital foods tablets were issued, which did help.

Bayeux had been taken on the first day and, some little while after a firm bridgehead had been secured, a mobile bath unit was set up in the city. This was indeed a great treat. Troops were taken by lorry into Bayeux and given the luxury of a shower and clean clothes. With so many troops involved in the landings I'm afraid this only happened to most of them once but nevertheless it was a very pleasant diversion.

The going was very hard and the Germans were determined to hold on in Normandy. Many battles were fought and many lives lost before the enemy was driven from Normandy and the flight across France, Belgium and Holland took place.

Looking back after all these years it was a wonderful piece of work to organise such a momentous undertaking and to keep such a vast amount of men supplied with everything that is needed to keep an army going.

I am glad I was part of it all and each time I return it is to remember those gallant lads who didn't make it. May they rest in peace.

CHAPTER SEVEN

THE REMAINS OF D-DAY IN HAMPSHIRE

Michael Hughes with introduction by Martin Doughty

As with most counties, the Second World War has left innumerable relics in the Hampshire environment. There was, of course, considerable devastation, principally in the major cities which, with the effects of subsequent post-war reconstuction, has fundamentally altered the fabric of Portsmouth and Southampton. In some cases actual ruins remain, preserved as monuments to the ordeals which created them. More frequently the impact of war is identified by subtle – or not so subtle – examples of rebuilding or by land-use which reflects the destruction of earlier buildings and the changed demands of late-twentieth-century life.

Moreover, as other chapters have made clear, the county has long been accustomed to a substantial military and naval presence which has left physical remains, some of very considerable size, distributed widely throughout Hampshire towns and countryside. Some of these installations remain in use for their original purposes today, others have been long abandoned or turned to alternative employment. But, beyond this, the innumerable more or less specialised installations created to prosecute the war have left their mark. Preparations for defence against a possible invasion, airfields and air defence installations, slipways, jetties and moorings all indicate the vast effort which was expended in fighting the war. Additionally, the need to support the fighting services has left indelible evidence on the Hampshire countryside: the Micheldever complex is just one reminder of the priorities of wartime and of the sacrifices which might have been bitterly contested in peace but which were made unhesitatingly in the face of national emergency.

This book, however, is not about the Second World War itself but about one episode within it, albeit a singularly important one. Compared with the general remains of war, the physical evidence in Hampshire which relates specifically to D-Day is much more restricted in scope. Nonetheless, it would be beyond the bounds of a single chapter to deal with it in detail, and other chapters have already drawn attention to many sites and monuments which remain. Some of these are major monuments in their own right, such as the dockyard at Portsmouth, and have a long history of which D-Day is only a part. In other cases, such as Southwick House, the role assumed in D-Day was of such central importance as to overshadow earlier history. But in all these cases, D-Day was only part of a wider story which cannot be told here.

Instead, this chapter focuses on sites which were specifically created to assist in the mounting of OVERLORD. Foremost in this category are the surviving remains of the construction sites for the MULBERRY harbours, perhaps Hampshire's single most important industrial contribution to the success of the operation. None of the component parts themselves remain in Hampshire (though there are remains on the Normandy coast) but extensive facilities and installations were necessary to build the harbours and much of this may still be seen.

The next chapter provides a photographic insight into the wealth of material preserved at the D-Day Museum in Portsmouth. Hampshire is the only county possessing a museum specifically dedicated to the commemoration of D-Day.

D-DAY ARCHAEOLOGY

Michael Hughes describes construction sites for the MULBERRY harbours in Hampshire.

"A headache for British Industry ...
A challenge to British labour ...
To engineers and contractors –
to clerks and to managers –
to foremen and chargehands –
to skilled men and labourers ...
To construct and assemble –
in six months from now –
Phoenix –
Gooseberry –
Bombardon –
Whale."

(excerpts from BBC Radio production 'The Harbour called Mulberry' first broadcast March 1945).

The pre-fabricated harbours which were used in the D-Day OVERLORD and NEPTUNE operations to provide shelter and landing facilities for vessels, troops and machinery during the invasion of German-occupied France were codenamed

PHOENIX caissons carrying anti-aircraft guns (IWM)

MULBERRY and comprised a number of different component parts with different functions. These included deep water shipping breakwaters codenamed BOMBARDON, floating pierhead units and roadways codenamed WHALE, temporary in-shore breakwaters consisting of scuttled ships codenamed GOOSEBERRY and permanent in-shore breakwaters consisting of concrete caissons codenamed PHOENIX, which when sunk provided support for the pierheads and the floating roadways.

The mass construction of the components of MULBERRY did not begin until December 1943, so that there was less than six months in which to complete the basic requirements for the D-Day landings. It was calculated that a labour force of 30,000 men would be required immediately. Fortunately the construction of camps, runways, and other installations connected with the mounting of Operation OVERLORD had by now been largely completed so that the organisation evolved by the Ministry of Works to keep track of allocations of men for particular jobs could now be adapted for the MULBERRY programme. Recruits were encouraged to move to areas like London and the South coast by the offers of accommodation, travelling allowances and other inducements. Ernest Bevin, Minister of Labour,

Type B2 PHOENIX under construction on a beach site (IWM)

took a close personal interest in the scheme, smoothing out problems with the unions and ensuring that the varying skills of the workforce would be used to the best advantage. Within 16 weeks over 25,000 men had been transferred to build MULBERRY components. When construction reached its peak a total of 45,000 men would be employed.

Apart from building some of the concrete caissons in existing docks, like Portsmouth Dockyard, some were built on beaches. Six sections of the PHOENIX harbours were constructed at Stone Point, near Lepe, whilst others were built at Hayling Island, where the remains of the construction site can be seen near the Eastney-Hayling ferry and at Stokes Bay, Gosport, where very little evidence of the construction sites survives today. Other MULBERRY harbour components were built on the banks of the Beaulieu River, at Marchwood, in Southampton Docks and on the sea-front at Southsea.

A total of 147 PHOENIX caissons of six different types were then towed across the Channel in the days following D-Day and strategically sunk off the Normandy coast at Arromanches and St Laurent. The remains of some of the caissons can still be seen on the beach and off-shore at Arromanches.

The caissons reinforced the temporary GOOSEBERRY blockship breakwaters which were installed during the initial landings, as the latter could be brought across the Channel under their own power more quickly than the PHOENIX units which had to be towed by tugs at a speed of 4–4.5 knots. The PHOENIX breakwaters were reinforced in the autumn of 1944 by the addition of supplementary strengthened caissons when it became apparent that they were to continue in use longer than the 90 days originally planned.

The type B2 caissons that were built at the three construction sites (as distinct from those constructed in Portsmouth Dockyard and elsewhere in South-East England), measured

Hayling Island PHOENIX construction (IWM)

62 m long, 14.3 m wide and 10.7 m high. They were divided into 22 compartments arranged in two rows of eleven separated by dividing concrete walls 0.3 m thick at intervals of 5 m. These were to provide stability during sinking. Gangways 1.8 m wide were provided around the sides and end of the caissons about 6 m below their top to carry scaffolding during construction, bollards for towing and holes for pumping out water during refloating operations. The caissons were made

of concrete slabs and assembled by a largely unskilled labour force. The type B2 did not carry anti-aircraft guns and only the sections at either end were roofed over with horizontal concrete slabs.

In the absence of a dry dock or facilities for building the caissons while floating, the assembled units were launched into the sea sideways. This operation was carried out when the units had been assembled to a height of about 6 m and weighed 2,000 tons. They were then completed while afloat, towed away and 'parked' on the seabed at Selsey or Dungeness until needed, when they were refloated ready for towing to Normandy.

The work at Stone Point was carried out by Wilson Lovatt and Sons Limited with technical assistance from Messrs Holloway Brothers (London) Limited who had developed the basic techniques used in the construction and sideways launching of heavy craft during work on a prototype alternative at Conway, in North Wales. Lovatt's employed approximately 700 men to carry out the construction work, whilst at Stokes Bay 13 caissons were manufactured by Holloway Brothers and Messrs W. C. French with a combined labour force of 1,400. At Hayling Island the construction of four PHOENIX units was undertaken by a labour force of 600 men for Messrs Trevor Construction Limited.

Stone Point, Lepe: concrete platform (M. Hughes)

Stone Point, Lepe (M. Hughes)

Slipways, Stone Point, Lepe (M. Hughes)

A recent detailed survey by the Royal Commission on Historical Monuments (England), undertaken on behalf of Hampshire County Council, has recorded the location of the surviving elements of the PHOENIX caisson construction site at Stone Point. The MULBERRY harbour construction site and D-Day embarkation site remains fall into three main spatial and functional areas on the beach. The northern half of the area is occupied by a long, raised, concrete and brick platform and associated features where the PHOENIX caissons were assembled. Immediately south of the end of the platform are the slipways and winch-house foundations used to launch the caissons sideways into the sea at high tide. The third part of the site comprises the remains of the concrete hardstandings, beach hardening mats and jetties used for the embarkation of the troops and vehicles taking part in the D-Day landings.

The survey reveals that the structure and function of most of the remaining fixed parts can be ascertained with a high degree of certainty. For example, the dimensions and structure of the long, raised, brick and concrete built platform demonstrated that it represented the remains of keel-block walls and a level base on which the caissons were assembled. This platform was raised to a height of approximately 2 m above the ground in order to leave sufficient space for the construction and operation of the mechanisms used to manoeuvre the caissons to the launching point. The total length of the platform (375 m or 1,230 ft) was adequate to accommodate six caissons arranged end to end and would have allowed all of the caissons built at Stone Point to be under construction at the same time (owing to the short amount of time available for the completion of the units, concurrent construction of them was essential).

Other features at Stone Point are the remains of the standing ways and mechanisms used to manoeuvre the caissons into the sea. (This operation is described in detail by Wilson and Sully.) The concrete slipways, whose remains today can be seen, especially at low tide, formed sloping standing ways down which the caissons were launched. Each assembled caisson was manoeuvred along the rolling track beyond the end of the construction platform until it lay directly above the slipway. The caissons were then transferred to a rolling track on the sliding ways before being launched sideways into the sea at high tide.

The extent to which the site was used subsequent to the completion of the MULBERRY operations is unclear but the Solent area was the scene of much activity throughout the war, including the pipeline under the Channel (PLUTO) which extended, eventually, all the way to Germany from a point near Lepe.

Stone Point was clearly not abandoned once construction had ceased; most of the non-fixed easily removable or iron component parts are no longer visible and can be assumed to have been removed. These not only include easily re-usable items such as scaffolding, much of the rolling track and the engines and winches used to provide motive power, but also more specialised items such as the mobile ball carriages and sliding ways on which the caissons were moved and the superstructures of the manoeuvring, launching and holding gear.

In April 1946, RAF air photographs reveal that many of the buildings within the area of the construction workers camp were still present and the embarkation jetty was still intact. In addition, some of the structures lying immediately on the landward side of the launching site and others alongside the construction platform are visible. This evidence suggests that the area continued in use in some form until after the end of the Second World War.

Also visible on air photographs are four PHOENIX caissons lying some 600 metres offshore in the Solent. Whilst these, which are roofed over and apparently carrying anti-aircraft guns, are evidently not

Concrete mats, Stone Point, Lepe (M. Hughes)

examples of the B2 type built at Stone Point, they do provide a vivid reminder of the purpose for which the surviving remains at Lepe were originally constructed, although they have long since disappeared from the offshore coast.

Although photographic records (held by Imperial War Museum, London) survive of the construction of the PHOENIX caissons at Hayling Island and Stokes Bay, preliminary research, to date, has failed to reveal any documentary sources for the three beach-side locations.

There is, however, a human glimpse of the labour force involved in the construction programme at the Stone Point site gleaned from an

examination of the relevant (1944 to 1946) Cadland Estate letter books made possible by the kind permission of Maldwin Drummond. For example, a letter of complaint from the Estate to Wilson Lovatt dated March 1944 concerns the men employed on contract who are being caught trespassing on a daily basis in the Estate's woods and copses and laying snares. Two other letters, dated February 1944, again from the Estate to the construction company, complain of damage to the bathing hut, the poaching and the stealing of chickens by the labour force!

The size of the other MULBERRY harbour components often involved construction methods similar to the

'Dolphins', Stone Point, Lepe (M. Hughes)

caissons. Twelve of the large pontoons were built for example, by Messrs Wates at Marchwood and Beaulieu. Fortunately, that winter was a mild one and favoured work out of doors. At Beaulieu, oyster beds were converted into dry docks by cleaning out and then concreting the bottoms.

The southern-most part of the site at Stone Point contains the remains of structures and fittings used to facilitate the embarkation of troops, equipment and vehicles taking part in the Allied landings in Normandy. An area of concrete hardstanding lies immediately south of the caisson launching site. It is partially obscured by shingle and narrows at its south end into a concrete surfaced trackway. This joins up with a network of similar wartime trackways to the south-west. A raised concrete slipway extends from the edge of the hardstanding down to the beach to the low water line. Two bollards for securing vessels during loading survive on the edge of the hardstanding. On the seaward side of the hardstanding areas of concrete beach hardening mats are still present extending beyond the low water mark. These mats consist of prefabricated slabs with an indented gridded upper surface held in position at the edge of the hardstanding by a series of iron hooks. Concrete and brick foundations west of the hardstanding represent the remains of buildings and a water tower associated with the army unit in control of the embarkation and tanks. Two standing 'dolphins', iron structures, lying in the sea just below the low-water mark are the remains of jetties used to load vessels bound for France. Over 6,000 troops embarked at Stone Point prior to D-Day.

CHAPTER EIGHT

THE D-DAY MUSEUM COLLECTION IN PORTSMOUTH

Stephen Brooks, curator of the D-Day Museum and Overlord Embroidery,
describes a selection of the fascinating material in
the Museum's displays and archives.

The D-Day Museum, Portsmouth. In the background can be seen Henry VIII's historic Southsea Castle, built in 1544.

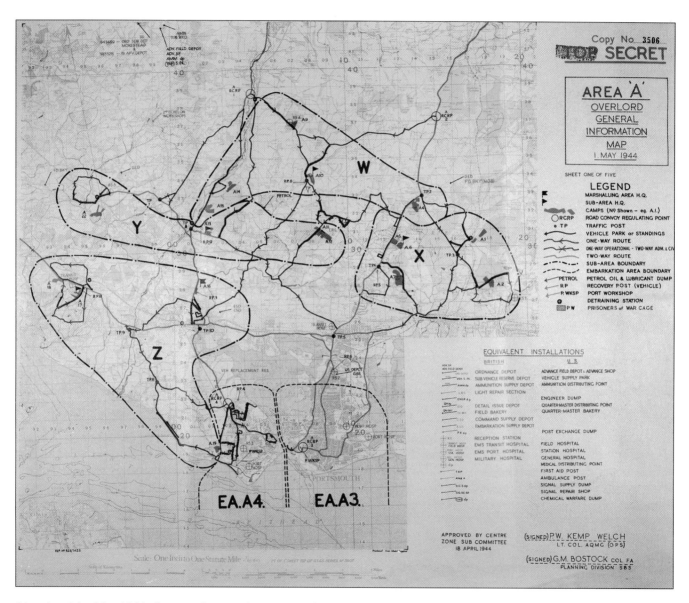

Map dated 1st May 1944, showing the complex system of traffic control, camps, workshops, depots, petrol dumps, hospitals and other facilities in the marshalling areas around Portsmouth harbour prior to D-Day.

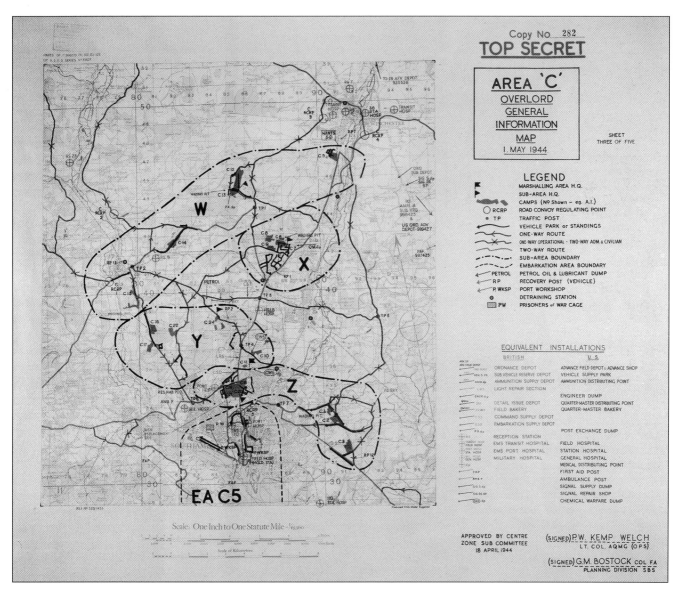

Map dated 1st May 1944, showing the complex system of traffic control, camps, workshops, depots, petrol dumps, hospitals and other facilities in the marshalling areas between Southampton and Winchester prior to D-Day.

Letter from Miss Norah Moffett of Holly Lodge, Droxford, to her aunt, describing the visit of the Prime Minister's special train to Droxford Station before D-Day:

'On the Friday before D-Day a special train came into Droxford Station and all the approaches to the Station were guarded by troops and guns. The train was drawn into the siding by the bridge we cross to go over the fields to the village and it had brought Mr Churchill, General Smuts and the chiefs of our armed forces and there was a conference with Eisenhower and Montgomery. Then the news that Rome had fallen came and the next thing we knew was that a War Cabinet meeting was being held in Droxford in the special train ... the whole place seemed alive with important personages. General Smuts and several of the ministers took walks through the village, but Mr Churchill was only seen taking his exercise along the railway in front of our house. In addition to all the 'big wigs' there were numerous black coated and smart lady secretaries. They <u>all</u> lived on the train which stayed from the Friday until the Sunday before D-Day. Mr Houghton – the little farmer living opposite us – was ordered to deliver milk to the train and each time he took it to the station an armed guard met him and escorted him along the track to the train. He was very proud of himself.'

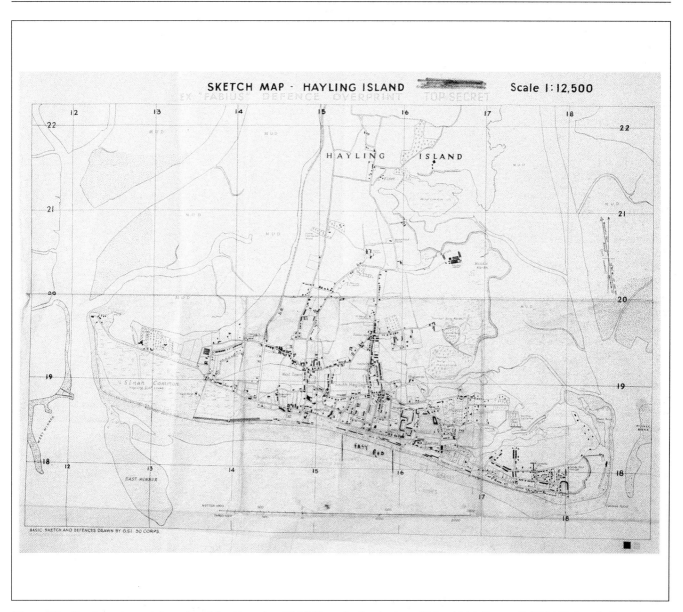

Map of Hayling Island specially printed for Exercise FABIUS at the beginning of May 1944. Force G (GOLD Beach, British 50th Infantry Division) practised its landing on the beaches of Hayling Island in preparation for D-Day.

Troops taking part in Exercise FABIUS, May 1944. The six component parts of FABIUS constituted the final exercise before D-Day itself, and involved the three British and Canadian assault forces in actual beach landings. Even at this late stage, valuable lessons were learnt which materially assisted the Allies' success on 6th June (IWM)

Troops embarking for Normandy along the scaffolding walkways linked to South Parade Pier, Southsea. Typical of the temporary structures thrown up to enable more or less dryshod transport of troops to the far shore, the Southsea arrangements also demonstrate the great difficulties faced in keeping military preparations and ordinary civilian life separate in the weeks leading up to D-Day (Portsmouth News)

Below: Personal Message from Rear-Admiral Talbot to Force S, which was to be responsible for landing the British 3rd Infantry Division on SWORD Beach on D-Day. The HQ for Force S was at Commercial Buildings in Portsmouth. Right: The unofficial 'Coat of Arms' which can be seen in the photograph of the Plotting Room at Fort Southwick is now on display at the D-Day Museum. It represents the link between the Plotting Room and the WAAFs in the RAF Stations round the coast. It was designed in 1944 by Miss C. P. Ward of the WRNS, who presented it to the Museum. Bottom right: Diagram of South Parade Pier, Southsea, drawn up at the time of Exercise FABIUS in May 1944 to show the proposed arrangements for embarking troops from the pier along specially constructed scaffolding walkways.

TO ALL IN FORCE "S"

The great day for which we have all been training is at hand. The task allotted to us is a formidable one, and calls for all that is best in every one of us.

The 3rd British Infantry Division has been entrusted to our care. They are old friends of ours; we have grown up together; we have come to look on them as our own. Let every officer and man in the Force feel a personal responsibility for the comfort, safety and maintenance of his "opposite number" in the 3rd Division.

And, above all FIGHT;
FIGHT to help the Army;
FIGHT to help yourselves;
FIGHT to save your ship;
FIGHT to the very end.

A. G. TALBOT,
Rear Admiral.

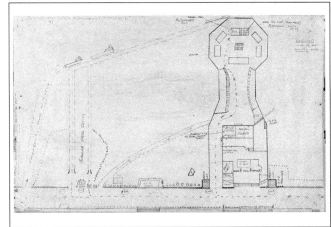

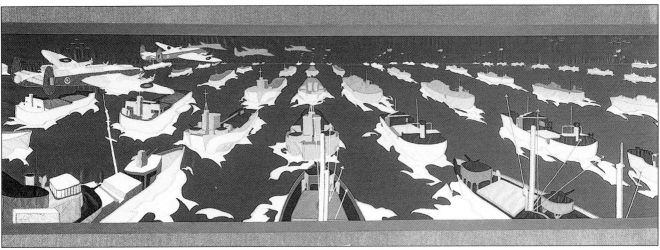

Top: In Panel 11 of the Overlord Embroidery, British troops on board their landing craft in a south coast port wait for the invasion of Normandy to be launched. To pass the time they study, with some amusement, the guidebook to France issued to the invasion forces.

Above: Centrepiece of Portsmouth's D-Day Museum is the 272-foot long Overlord Embroidery, a modern counter- part to the Bayeux Tapestry. It was commissioned by Lord Dulverton in 1968, and worked by the Royal School of Needlework, to the designs of Miss

Sandra Lawrence, over the following five years. Panel 13, illustrated here, shows the Allied invasion forces streaming down the mineswept corridors from the assembly area – 'Piccadilly Circus' – south of the Isle of Wight towards the Normandy beaches.

RESTRICTED

MARSHALLING AREA "S"

MARSHALLING ORDERS FOR UNIT PARTY COMDS

1. You will remain in comd of this unit party until relieved on the other side.

2. Your tps will require in Camp :—
   - (a) Full marching order.
   - (b) Arms.
   - (c) Blankets.

3. Your guide will inform you :—
   - (a) Whether a guard or the dvrs will remain on the vehs.
   - (b) The method of moving to Camp.

4. All tps are confined to Camp.

5. You will later be called to a conference at the Sub Area HQ at which your OC Tps will be appointed and under whose comd you will then be.

6. You will ensure that all ranks know what to do in the event of :—
   - (a) Fire.
   - (b) Air attack.
   - (c) Butterfly bomb attack.
   - (d) Ground attack.
   - (e) Gas attack.

7. **Waterproofing.**—You will receive orders as to the completion of waterproofing.

8. **Documentation.**—You will prepare accurately AFs W.5169 for parties over 5 and vehs, and 3060 for parties under 5 without vehs. Two copies of AF W.3060 are required and 4 copies of AF W.5169. One copy of AF W.3060 and 3 copies of AF W.5169 will be subsequently collected by OC Tps.

Above: Marshalling orders for Area S to the north of Portsmouth, where the British 3rd Infantry Division, destined for SWORD Beach on D-Day, was encamped.
Top right: Pass to the Underground Headquarters at Fort Southwick, issued to Third Officer M. N. Rodwell, WRNS.
Right: Personal Message to troops issued by General Sir Bernard Montgomery, Commander-in-Chief, 21st Army Group, signed and dated on the eve of D-Day. This copy of the message was presented to the D-Day Museum by Viscount Montgomery, the Field Marshal's son, to mark the occasion of the one-millionth visit to the Museum in November 1990.

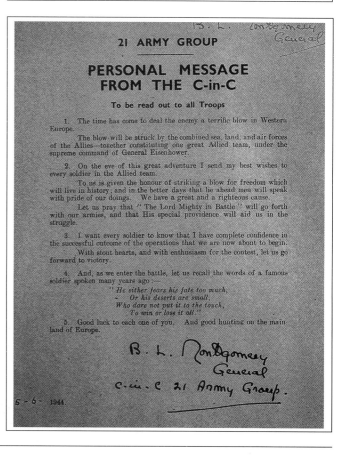

No. 7279

HEADQUARTERS PASS

Name ... M. N. Rodwell

Rank or Rating ... 3/o W.R.N.S.

No. of Identity Card or Pay Book ... 15109

Branch ... N.O.M.

Signature of Holder ...

Pass admits to Headquarters not crossed out

A B C D E ~~F~~ ~~G~~ H

B. L. Montgomery
General

21 ARMY GROUP

PERSONAL MESSAGE FROM THE C-in-C

To be read out to all Troops

1. The time has come to deal the enemy a terrific blow in Western Europe.
   The blow will be struck by the combined sea, land, and air forces of the Allies—together constituting one great Allied team, under the supreme command of General Eisenhower.

2. On the eve of this great adventure I send my best wishes to every soldier in the Allied team.
   To us is given the honour of striking a blow for freedom which will live in history; and in the better days that lie ahead men will speak with pride of our doings. We have a great and a righteous cause.
   Let us pray that "The Lord Mighty in Battle" will go forth with our armies, and that His special providence will aid us in the struggle.

3. I want every soldier to know that I have complete confidence in the successful outcome of the operations that we are now about to begin.
   With stout hearts, and with enthusiasm for the contest, let us go forward to victory.

4. And, as we enter the battle, let us recall the words of a famous soldier spoken many years ago :—
   "He either fears his fate too much,
   Or his deserts are small,
   Who dare not put it to the touch,
   To win or lose it all."

5. Good luck to each one of you. And good hunting on the mainland of Europe.

B. L. Montgomery
General
C-in-C 21 Army Group.

5-6-1944.

As part of the immense efforts put into the preparation for D-Day, both British and American forces produced guidebooks and phrasebooks to help the men get along with the French. In a section of Dos and Don'ts the British guide advised, 'Don't get into any arguments about religion or politics. If a Frenchman raises one of the points which have strained Anglo-French relations since 1940, drop the matter. There are two sides to every question, but you don't want to take either.'

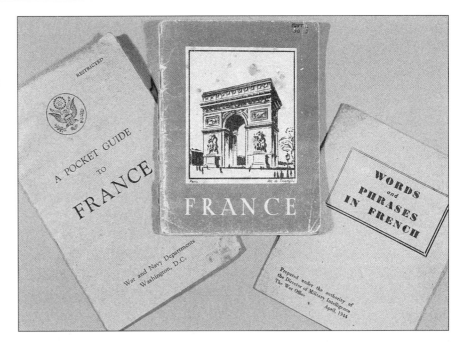

Staff in the Plotting Room at the Combined Operations headquarters for D-Day, 149 steps below Fort Southwick on Portsdown Hill. One Wren, Mary Howes, recalled that 'going down wasn't too bad, but coming up after a night duty was devastating.' (Portsmouth News).

Martin Doughty

Martin Doughty is an historian specialising in modern British history and with a life-long interest in military and, especially, naval history. He recently moved from Hampshire to Worcester, where he now works at the Worcester College of Higher Education.

Ken Ford

Ken Ford trained as an engineer with British Telecom, but is now a book dealer specialising in military books. He is the author of *Assault Crossing* and *Assault on Germany* and a member of the Fortress Study Group.

Martin Polley

Martin Polley teaches history at King Alfred's College Winchester. He gained his Ph.D. from the University of Wales in 1991, and previously worked as a historical research assistant in the Foreign and Commonwealth Office.

Alastair Wilson

Commander Alastair Wilson served for 34 years in the Royal Navy. Since 1984, he has been associated with the Historic Dockyards at both Portsmouth and Chatham. He also writes for professional journals.

Lesley Burton

Lesley Burton specialises in the history of Hampshire and, especially, Gosport. She has written extensively on the role of the county during the Second World War. She is also Chairman and Editor of the Gosport Society.

Ann Bailey

Ann Bailey works with the Winchester History Project at King Alfred's College, Winchester, which is tracing the history of Winchester properties from 1550 to the present day and creating a computerised database for researchers and the local community. She is also a member of the Ampfield Country-side Heritage Area Historical Group.

Michael Hughes

Michael Hughes, M.Phil, FSA, FRHist.S., MIFA is Hampshire County Archaeologist and Visiting Fellow of Southampton University. He is a lecturer and author currently working on a book on the origins of Hampshire.

Stephen Brooks

Stephen Brooks worked at the Imperial War Museum for ten years before becoming Keeper of Military History and curator of the D-Day Museum at Portsmouth in 1987.

The list of books on D-Day is immense and growing all the time. The following list refers to published sources specifically used in the preparation of this book, or specifically relevant to Hampshire. Unpublished sources for D-Day are similarly numerous. The main collections may be found in the Imperial War Museum, London and the Public Record Office, Kew. Newspapers and periodicals, available from local record offices, are another rich source.

Ashton P. & K.
Hampshire and the United States
1986
Ashworth C.
Action Stations 5
1982
Ashworth C.
Action Stations 9
1985
Barnett G. E.
City of Portsmouth Records of the Corporation, 1936-1945
Belchem D.
All in the Day's March
1978

Bradley O.
A Soldier's Story
1951
Burton L. A.
D-Day: Our Great Enterprise
1984
Burton L. A.
Gosport goes to War
1981
Burton L. A. & Musselwhite B.
An Illustrated History of Fareham
1991
Calder A.
The People's War: Britain 1939-1945
1971
Darwin B.
War On The Line: the story of the Southern Railway in war-time including D-Day on the Southern
1946
De Guingand F.
Operation Victory
1947
Edwards K. E.
Operation Neptune
1946
Eisenhower D.
Eisenhower at War, 1943-1945
1986
Eisenhower D. D.

Crusade in Europe
1948
Ellis L. F.
Victory in the West, Vol 1
1962
Fairman J. R.
Netley Hospital and its Railways
1984
Hamilton N.
Monty: Master of the Battlefield
1983
Hancock, W. K. & Gowing, M. M.
The British War Economy
1949
Hartcup G.
Code Name Mulberry: the planning, building and operation of the Normandy harbours
1977
Hastings M.
Overlord: D-Day and the Battle for Normandy
1984
Hodge W. J.
'The Mulberry Invasion Harbours – their design, preparation and installation' in *The Structural Engineer* March 1946
Hughes M. & Lewis C.
'The Archaeology of D-Day: the

remains at Stone Point, Lepe' in
Archaeology in Hampshire
1990

Hughes M. F.
The Archaeology of D-Day
1992

Kemp A.
Springboard for Overlord:
Hampshire and the D-Day Landings
1984

Kemp A.
Southampton at War 1939-45
1989

Knowles B.
Southampton: The English Gateway
1951

Ladd J. D.
Assault from the Sea, 1939-1945
1976

Lipscombe F. W.
D-Day Story
1965

Lipscombe F. W.
Heritage of Sea Power
1967

Lund P. & Ludlam H.
The War of the Landing Craft
1976

Morgan F. E.
Overture to Overlord

1950

Morison S. E.
Invasion of France and Germany,
1944-1945
1957

O'Connell G.
Southwick, the D-Day Village
1984

Postan M. M.
British War Production
1952

Pothecary R.
Yanks at Southampton: the 14th
Major Port of Transportation Corps
of the United States Army in
Hampshire, 1943-45
1986

Robertson K.
Eastleigh: a Railway Town
1992

Roskill S. W.
The War at Sea, Vol. III part II
1961

Schofield B. B.
Operation Neptune
1974

Stagg J. M.
Forecast for Overlord
1971

Temple Patterson A.

Southampton: a biography
1970

Tute W., Costello J. & Hughes T.
D-Day
1974

Waller J. & Vaughan-Rees M.
Women in Uniform 1939-1945

Webb J., Quail S., Haskell P. & Riley R.
The Spirit of Portsmouth: a history
1989

White I.
The Story of Gosport
1989

Wilmot C.
The Struggle for Europe
1952

Wilson W. S. & Sully F. W.
'The Traversing and Side-Launching
of Heavy Craft' in *Proceedings of the*
Conference on Wartime Engineering
Problems, Institute of Civil Engineers
June 1947

Winton J.
The Naval Heritage of Portsmouth
1989

Wood R. J.
'Phoenix' in *Proceedings of the*
Conference on Wartime Engineering
Problems, Institute of Civil Engineers
June 1947

AA	Anti-Aircraft	PLUTO	Pipeline, Underwater Transport of Oil	
ALG	Advanced Landing Ground	POL	Petrol, Oil and Lubricants	
ATS	Auxiliary Transport Service	RAF	Royal Air Force	
BEF	British Expeditionary Force	REC	Railway Executive Committee	
BUCO	Build-Up Control Organisation	RNAS	Royal Naval Air Service	
COSSAC	Chief of Staff to the Supreme Allied Commander	RNVR	Royal Naval Volunteer Reserve	
DD	Duplex Drive	SHAEF	Supreme Headquarters, Allied Expeditionary Force	
ENSA	Entertainments National Service Association	SLUG	Surf Landing Under Girder	
LCA	Landing Craft (Assault)	TURCO	Turn-Round Control Organisation	
LCI	Landing Craft (Infantry)	USAAF	United States Army Air Force	
LCT	Landing Craft (Tank)			
LCT(R)	Landing Craft Tank (Rocket)	WRNS	Women's Royal Naval Service	
LST	Landing Ship (Tank)	WVS	Women's Voluntary Service	
LSWR	London and South Western Railway			
MGB	Motor Gun Boat			
ML	Motor Launch			
MTB	Motor Torpedo Boat			
NAAFI	Navy, Army and Air Force Institutes			
NDLC	National Docks Labour Corporation			

PICTURE CREDITS

ABP Southampton	Associated British Ports (Southampton)
ENHT	Evening News and Hampshire Telegraph
HC	Hampshire Chronicle
HJC	Hallett Jerrard Collection
IWM	Imperial War Museum
PCS	Portsmouth City Secretariat